Cambridge Elements

Elements in Criminology
edited by
David Weisburd
George Mason University, Virginia
Hebrew University of Jerusalem

THE HIDDEN MEASUREMENT CRISIS IN CRIMINOLOGY

Procedural Justice as a Case Study

Amanda Graham
Texas State University
Francis T. Cullen
University of Cincinnati
Bruce G. Link
University of California, Riverside

Shaftesbury Road, Cambridge CB2 8EA, United Kingdom

One Liberty Plaza, 20th Floor, New York, NY 10006, USA

477 Williamstown Road, Port Melbourne, VIC 3207, Australia

314–321, 3rd Floor, Plot 3, Splendor Forum, Jasola District Centre, New Delhi – 110025, India

103 Penang Road, #05–06/07, Visioncrest Commercial, Singapore 238467

Cambridge University Press is part of Cambridge University Press & Assessment, a department of the University of Cambridge.

We share the University's mission to contribute to society through the pursuit of education, learning and research at the highest international levels of excellence.

www.cambridge.org
Information on this title: www.cambridge.org/9781009558556

DOI: 10.1017/9781009558549

First published 2025

A catalogue record for this publication is available from the British Library

ISBN 978-1-009-55855-6 Hardback
ISBN 978-1-009-55856-3 Paperback
ISSN 2633-3341 (online)
ISSN 2633-3333 (print)

Additional resources for this publication at www.cambridge.org/Graham

The Hidden Measurement Crisis in Criminology

Procedural Justice as a Case Study

Elements in Criminology

DOI: 10.1017/9781009558549
First published online: February 2025

Amanda Graham
Texas State University

Francis T. Cullen
University of Cincinnati

Bruce G. Link
University of California, Riverside

Author for correspondence: Amanda Graham, akg79@txstate.edu

Abstract: The field of criminology is limited by a "hidden" measurement crisis. It is hidden because scholars either are not aware of the shortcomings of their measures or have implicitly agreed that scales with certain properties merit publication. It is a crisis because the approaches used to construct measures do not employ modern systematic psychometric methods. As a result, the degree to which existing measures have methodological limitations is unknown. The purpose of this Element is to unmask this hidden crisis and provide a case study demonstrating how to build a measure of a prominent criminological construct through modern systematic psychometric methods. Using multiple surveys and item response theory, it develops a 10-item scale of procedural justice in policing. This scale can be used in primary research and to adjudicate existing measures. The goal is to reveal the nature of the field's measurement crisis and show a strategy for solving it.

Keywords: criminometrics, procedural justice, measurement, policing, item response theory

ISBNs: 9781009558556 (HB), 9781009558563 (PB), 9781009558549 (OC)
ISSNs: 2633-3341 (online), 2633-3333 (print)

Contents

1 Introduction

The field of criminology faces a hidden measurement crisis – hidden because most scholars, prominent and otherwise, do not know or acknowledge that it exists. As will be explained, this hidden crisis is that virtually all measures in the field are not constructed systematically. The approaches used to develop measures in criminology, including of core constructs, do not employ state-of-the-art psychometric methods.

Crime scholars thus are unaware that their measures may be flawed. But they are not troubled; ignorance is bliss. They can claim methodological rigor by employing normative "best practices." Although unwritten, the ruling criteria are well understood and transmitted to new scholars through occupational socialization. These include using items with face validity, a scale with an alpha of 0.70 or higher, and factor analysis of items to ensure they have strong factor loadings. A preference exists for scales with five or more items, but especially in secondary data analysis where options are limited, two- and three-item scales can be published in leading journals and iconic books. This social construction of what constitutes "good measurers" is hegemonic and virtually unquestioned.

Indeed, these standards inform the work of researchers and journal reviewers alike. But no incentive exists for scholars to use more rigorous methods of measurement. Doing so would potentially require multiple surveys and complex item analysis. Maintaining the status quo, moreover, can be justified by citing prior studies using the same measures. The possibility that the blind may be leading the blind is not considered.

We include ourselves among the "blind." We have been fortunate to have had productive academic careers. During this time – a half century for the second (Cullen) and third (Link) authors – we employed the same approach to measurement "as everyone else." It took the first author (Graham) to question this approach and to prompt us to initiate a call for a fresh strategy. This Element is thus an exercise in self-criticism and an indictment of current ways of constructing measures. We embark on this task not with false hubris but with justified humility.

As a result of all of this, the degree to which existing measures have methodological limitations is unknown. Two negative consequences follow. First, in many areas, several different scales have been used to measure the same concept. The resulting heterogeneity in measures creates a situation in which it is difficult to determine if divergent findings or low explained variance are due to substantive factors or are measurement-related artifacts.

Second, it is difficult to accumulate knowledge when no agreed-upon standard measure exists in an area. For example, despite a vast literature on Hirschi's (1969) social bond theory, studies have yielded conflicting findings that inhibit a definitive evaluation of the theory's empirical status (Kempf, 1993; Kempf-Leonard, 2019). A key culprit in this frustrating conclusion is the use of diverse measures of each of the four bonds that undermines the accumulation of knowledge.

In this context, the purpose of this Element is twofold. The first purpose is to elucidate the hidden crisis and to explain its nature and consequences. Section 2 is devoted to this task. Evidence is presented to exemplify the limits of existing measurement in the literature. The second purpose is to present a strategy for addressing the crisis. Section 2 initiates this discussion by conveying how quality measures are built through psychometrics, making the case that this approach should be applied in criminology. That is, we call for the invention of the specialty of *criminometrics* – psychometrics in the context of criminology and criminal justice.

To illuminate the steps and value of this method, we then move beyond critique to action to exemplify the proposed approach to measurement. As a case study, we created a measure of procedural justice, which is rooted in the work of Tyler and others and includes a rich line of research in policing. As scholars have noted, assessing the impact of procedural justice has been limited by studies using diverse measures of the construct (Mazerolle, Bennett, et al., 2013). Section 3 reviews the intellectual history of the concept of procedural justice.

In Section 4, a case study is undertaken to measure procedural justice. Psychometric methods are employed to distill from a large pool of items a 10-item measure of procedural justice. This scale has practical value in that it can be incorporated into future studies of procedural justice. The intent is that due to its strong properties, this measure will become standard in the field. If so, its repeated use will facilitate the accumulation of knowledge.

But another benefit exists. We are not arguing that all measures in the field are flawed. Even in the absence of psychometric methods, some scholars might have a knack for developing very good scales. The difficulty at present is that discerning the good, the bad, and the ugly among a concept's multiple measures is not achieved easily and without dispute among each scale's advocates. However, given their strong psychometric properties, new scales developed in this manner – such as our measure – can help settle the matter. They can be used as a barometer for assessing the quality of the existing measures of a concept and thus for adjudicating their relative merits. Section 5 is devoted to showing how this might be done.

The Element ends in Section 6 with a call for scholars to take measurement seriously and embrace criminometrics. With the example of measuring procedural justice provided, other researchers can follow this template, embarking on studies that use criminometric methods to develop measures of all criminological concepts. If our work inspires this line of inquiry, it promises to have a transformative effect on the quality of criminological research. Indeed, a turning point in criminology is in the offing.

2 The Measurement Crisis in Criminology

Scholars universally recognize that quality science depends on quality measurement. In their training, students must take methods courses, where the importance of valid and reliable measures is preached. Whole sections of research manuscripts are dedicated to presenting and justifying scientific methods and measurement of constructs. Ultimately, the quality of the manuscript is evaluated based on whether the measures are seen to capture empirical reality and avoid methodological artifacts.

As will be explained in Section 4, the extant normative standards in criminology and criminal justice used to evaluate the quality of measures are based on classical test theory. However, advancements in measurement (e.g., item response theory) and the systematic development of measures for core constructs have not been adopted in criminology and criminal justice. What are the consequences? Public policy and criminal justice practices advanced by measures used in evaluating theory and practice rest on a potentially shaky foundation of constructs measured in unsystematic and less-than-rigorous methods. As such, these measures may be flawed, less than ideal, or incomplete in measuring core criminological constructs. Therefore, the conclusions reached are also potentially flawed or incomplete. When the foundational aspect of science – measurement – is called into question, a crisis exists. When research continues to use unsystematic measurement methods despite better methodologies, this is a systemic and patterned crisis. When scholars are unaware of the crisis, it is hidden.

A pressing need exists in criminology to recognize and systematically address this hidden measurement crisis. This crisis involves the lack of clear, consistent conceptualization and operationalization of its constructs across the field. Currently, most constructs are measured by various measures consisting of differing items and numbers of items. When using secondary data sets, scholars developing new constructs must, ad hoc, rely on available items to capture the concept of interest. Even when collecting primary data, scholars typically invent their own measures, combining items with face validity and acceptable alpha scores. Alternatively, primary data scholars are left unsystematically vetting the current literature to use a measure published by someone else. More extensive and effective psychometric methods – what we call "criminometrics" – are not employed.

Defenders of the existing measurement order can retort that they can point to measures with face validity and good metrics (alphas, factor loadings) that explain variation across studies and contexts. We do not dispute this reality. Existing scales developed by thoughtful scholars might have value and, if so, should be retained as a measurement option. But here is the challenge. First, without measures developed systematically and rigorously, it is unknowable whether a superior scale is possible. Second, among existing measures, it is unknowable which are effective and which are deeply flawed. Third, when multiple scales exist to measure a single construct (such as procedural justice), it is unknowable which one a scholar should select when undertaking a new study. Separating the wheat from the chaff requires measures developed systematically and with the most rigorous criteria.

Dictionaries generally define a crisis as a "decisive moment," "a situation that has reached a critical phase" (Merriam-Webster, 2025), or "a situation in which something … is affected by one or more serious problems" (Collins, 2025). Our thesis is that measurement within criminology is in such a troubling situation, made all the worse because its existence and consequences are not recognized. A crisis, however, comes with a silver lining, making possible a "turning point" in which a different road can be taken that lessens or eliminates the crisis. This Element seeks to inspire a measurement turning point in the field.

Thus, this Element serves as a case study in "criminometrics." In so doing, the strategy is to follow the methods used more often in psychology for psychometric measurement of concepts, focusing on procedural justice in policing. As a prelude to this case study, this section will first reflect more fully on the hidden measurement crisis in criminology and then examine how measures in criminology and criminal justice should be developed.

2.1 The Problem: Measurement in Criminology

Currently, criminology has no requirements as to how measures of concepts should be built, evaluated, and validated. Unlike psychology, criminology's leading professional association, the American Society of Criminology, does not provide a guide or standards for the criminometric measurement of criminological concepts. Furthermore, the leading journals, such as *Criminology* and *Justice Quarterly*, do not require authors to report the details of the measurement of their constructs – a requirement of leading psychology journals, such as *Personality and Individual Differences* and *Psychological Bulletin*, and a recommendation of APA Style Journal Article Reporting Standards (JARS-Quant; APA, 2020). This lack of guidance or standards has led to high diversity of measures in criminology.

In one of the most widely used texts on measurement, DeVellis (2012) warns of the dangers of using measures not developed by any systematic scientific process. He states that "poor measurement imposes an absolute limit on the validity of the conclusions one can reach" (p. 15). More simply stated, any findings based on poorly measured constructs are qualified by the use of the specific measure developed by the authors. Additionally, there is a continued risk that findings depend solely upon the specified measures, not a true relationship between variables (DeVellis, 2012).

DeVellis (2012) further warns that when studies use diverse (and potentially flawed) measures of the same constructs, the results are difficult to compare. The risk is that mixed findings will continue to populate journals and knowledge will not accumulate to a meaningful conclusion (DeVellis, 2012). There is evidence of this problem, as seen in the stability of low explained variance in criminological studies over the past 40 years (Weisburd & Piquero, 2008). Clearly, criminology is facing a crisis in measurement that has yet to be fully acknowledged.

This state of affairs does not exist in psychology, which has a long and storied history of developing and prioritizing conceptual measures that date back to at least 200 BC in China (DuBois, 1970; Elman, 2013; Têng, 1943). In fact, the field of psychology itself was warned by Cattell (1890), who, at the time, stated boldly, "Psychology cannot attain the certainty and exactness of the physical sciences, unless it rests on a foundation of experiment and measurement" (p. 373). As will be argued, psychology's approach may serve as a template for criminology to develop its measures (DuBois, 1970).

Before continuing, we wish to add context to the following discussion and analysis. To elucidate the currently accepted approaches to scale development and subsequent measurement crisis, we present examples of preeminent scales. These examples are drawn from high-quality scholarly work. Our critiques are not to diminish the value of these contributions. Rather, our aim is specific: to use published works to demonstrate the existence of a measurement crisis – contemporary psychometric methods are currently not employed in criminology to develop measures of constructs.

2.2 The Solution: How Measures Should Be Developed

Leaders and organizations in psychology have detailed the standards for developing new psychological measures in books, manuals, and even journal articles. Although there is some diversity among these sources about the process of constructing a new measure, each describes a similar undertaking. The following content provides an overview of this methodology while incorporating several references that provide relevant details at various stages. In total, the measurement development process can be roughly distilled into six stages.

In the first stage, a construct needs to be defined as to what it is and what it is not (AERA et al., 2014; Clark & Watson, 1995; Dawis, 1987; DeVellis, 2012; Netemeyer et al., 2003; Simms, 2008; Spector, 1992; Tangney et al., 2004). Many scholars suggest using previous literature and theory to aid in defining a construct and its theoretical boundaries or distinctions from related constructs (AERA et al., 2014; Clark & Watson, 1995; Tangney et al., 2004). It is also important to examine past attempts at measurement to determine the process used to measure this construct successfully or unsuccessfully (Tangney et al., 2004).

In the second stage, a large pool of potential items is developed to measure this construct (AERA et al., 2014; Clark & Watson, 1995; Dawis, 1987; DeVellis, 2012; Loevinger, 1957; Netemeyer et al., 2003; Simms, 2008; Spector, 1992; Tangney et al., 2004). Using theory, previous literature, ethnographic research, interviews/panels with representative members of the target population, or other methods, a variety of survey items is developed (Dawis, 1987; Dillman et al., 2014). This pool of items may include similar questions with slightly different wording to attend to the influence of word choice on responses (AERA et al., 2014). For comparable reasons, items' response options or format may vary (AERA et al., 2014; Clark & Watson, 1995; Dawis, 1987; Dillman et al., 2014; Spector, 1992). For example, using a middle category (e.g., neither support nor oppose), which allows respondents to be indecisive, may not be ideal for measuring some constructs. In this stage, the administration of the test or survey (e.g., online, in person) is also determined (AERA et al., 2014). Alongside the pool of items developed, some researchers suggest the use of "anchor" or "comparison" scales to demarcate the boundaries of a construct (Clark & Watson, 1995). Also, including validation items is beneficial when examining social desirability bias in responses and construct validity in later steps of construct development (DeVellis, 2012). Finally, subject matter experts should review the pool of items to ensure the universe of items that could be used to measure this construct is represented. This improves the initial pool's content validity (DeVellis, 2012; Simms, 2008).

In the third stage, this pool of items is pilot tested with a sample, which would ideally be representative of the target population (AERA et al., 2014; Clark & Watson, 1995; Dawis, 1987; DeVellis, 2012; Loevinger, 1957; Netemeyer et al., 2003; Simms, 2008; Spector, 1992; Tangney et al., 2004). Representativeness here is consequential because a nonrepresentative pilot sample could lead to biased results, leading to the removal of items that would otherwise be relevant for measuring a construct (Netemeyer et al., 2003). In addition, the pilot sample size should be considered based on the dimensionality and complexity of a construct (Netemeyer et al., 2003). Clark and Watson (1995) believe a sample size of 300 is sufficient, but Netemeyer and colleagues (2003) suggest larger sample sizes for loosely defined or multidimensional constructs. In addition to testing the measurement tool on a smaller sample, this initial pilot test serves to identify early estimates of the reliability and validity of the measurement tool (Netemeyer et al., 2003). Furthermore, pilot testing can help reduce the number of items needed to measure a construct by identifying and discarding poorly performing items (Netemeyer et al., 2003).

In the fourth stage, which will be discussed in more detail in Section 4, the results of the pilot test are analyzed with the intent of developing a strong, more parsimonious tool that may become the finalized tool (AERA et al., 2014; Dawis, 1987; DeVellis, 2012; Simms, 2008; Spector, 1992; Tangney et al., 2004). Using classical test theory (CTT), exploratory factor analysis (EFA) is employed to reduce the number of items in a scale while maintaining the maximal explained variance and to locate an underlying dimensionality of a measure (Netemeyer et al., 2003). After EFA, confirmatory factor analysis (CFA) is often used to perform even more rigorous testing of the construct, including examining invariance and confirming factor structure (Netemeyer et al., 2003). More recently, item response theory (IRT) has provided a method of analyzing in more depth the contributions of items and their responses to the quality of the scale (Clark & Watson, 1995). These analyses aim to evaluate the convergent, discriminant, and criterion-related validity and the reliability of the items used to measure the construct (Simms, 2008). Throughout this process, the tool is revised to optimize length while maintaining the reliability and validity of the construct. In addition, this stage may include the development of provisional scales (Simms, 2008).

In the fifth stage, the revised pool of items is administered to another representative sample to examine the shorter scale's performance (Clark & Watson, 1995; Dawis, 1987; Loevinger, 1957; Spector, 1992; Tangney et al., 2004). After administering the tool, the same statistical analyses are completed to examine the reliability and validity of the tool. In this stage, if the tool is not performing as desired, the items can be modified based on the original pool of items, piloted, and reanalyzed until a measurement tool performs "well" based on modern psychometric methods and standards (Furr, 2011).

Finally, in the sixth stage, documentation for using the tool and the tool itself are copyrighted for outside use (AERA et al., 2014; Simms, 2008). This documentation includes instructions for using the tool, interpretation of results when used, and specifications for its use (AERA et al., 2014). Furthermore, the publication of the steps taken to develop the scale should be available for users to examine (AERA et al., 2014).

Although this process seems linear and quick, it can often be arduous, especially when piloting, revising, and validating the tool (Furr, 2011). Still, this psychometric process has been used to develop measures for more than 100 years and is supported by leading psychological and educational organizations (DuBois, 1970).

One caveat should be added. In psychology, relying on psychometrics to develop measures is well known and common. In fact, there is a journal devoted to this inquiry – *Psychometrika*. However, the quality of measurement varies in published works. Some works develop new measures psychometrically; others use existing scales constructed in this way. Still other published writings construct scales the way we do in criminology. The difference in psychology is that the best measurement practices are part of the field's knowledge base, are often employed in research, and offer a source of criticism when not used.

2.3 Measuring Concepts in Criminology: Two Examples

The previous two sections (1) have suggested that measurement within criminology and criminal justice is unsystematic and thus is problematic, and (2) have provided an overview of a promising method for addressing this measurement crisis, which exists in psychology. The current section aims to concretely illustrate the state of measurement in criminology and criminal justice. This task is pursued by assessing the measurement of two core constructs of leading theories of crime – microlevel self-control and macrolevel collective efficacy. These constructs are selected because they have had enormous impact on the field theoretically and substantively. Both perspectives, moreover, are measured regularly with scales developed roughly three decades ago. The developers of these scales were careful and innovative, but they did not use current psychometric methods. We argue that the time has come to do so.

2.3.1 Self-Control Theory as a Measurement Example

Development of the Grasmick et al. Scale

In 1990, Michael Gottfredson and Travis Hirschi published what would prove to be an iconic theoretical work, *A General Theory of Crime*. Their core proposition was that "criminality," or the propensity or tendency of individuals to commit criminal acts, is related to criminal involvement (Gottfredson & Hirschi, 1990, p. 85). This language is seemingly tautological about crime causation. Recognizing this fact, Gottfredson and Hirschi replaced the concept of criminality with the concept of self-control. They argued that low self-control had general effects positively and powerfully related to crime and deviance across all populations, in all contexts, and at all times in life.

In their chapter on "The Nature of Criminality," they set out to define self-control. In a discussion somewhat at odds with itself, Gottfredson and Hirschi argued that self-control was a unidimensional or individual propensity or predisposition. But they then inserted a section titled "The Elements of Self-Control," which described six features of the construct. Gottfredson and Hirschi (1990) concluded, "people who lack self-control will tend to be impulsive, insensitive, physical (as opposed to mental), risk-taking, short-sighted, and nonverbal, and they will tend therefore to engage in criminal and analogous acts" (p. 90).

Gottfredson and Hirschi's theory was theoretically magisterial and offered rich opportunities for empirical studies. Tests of this bold new theory required only two things: a measure of crime and a measure of self-control. Different scholars took up this challenge, but one group offered a compelling measure of self-control. Along with Charles Tittle, Robert Bursik, and Bruce Arneklev, Harold Grasmick (1993) sought, as the title of his article read, to test "the core empirical implications of Gottfredson and Hirschi's General Theory of Crime." Their sample was limited – 395 adults responding to the annual Oklahoma City Survey – and their measure of crime was weak (incidents of force or fraud in the past five years). By contrast, Grasmick et al. delved deeply into the concept of low self-control and created a scale of enduring influence.

In their 1993 article, Grasmick et al. (1993) briefly reviewed how they developed their scale. They first considered the 38-item self-control subscale of the California Psychology Inventory, but they rejected its use because it did not capture the peculiar description of self-control offered by Gottfredson and Hirschi (p. 13). They then turned to the section in *A General Theory of Crime* on "the elements of self-control." "We chose," they disclosed, "to develop our own measure of the six components, following as closely as possible Gottfredson and Hirschi's descriptions of them" (p. 13). Their goal was to have a 24-item multidimensional scale, with 4 items used for each of the six elements. These items are listed in Table 1.

Notably, Grasmick et al. (1993) engaged in some psychometrically valuable strategies. For example, in developing their scale, "various combinations of items were pretested on several samples of college students" to select items that had "sufficient variances" and "that tended to be unidimensional in their factor structure" (p. 13). Based on the responses from their Oklahoma City Survey, they employed factor analysis to identify and report on the six subscales of "self-control," operationalizing them as a single unidimensional construct (Grasmick et al., 1993). Furthermore, using regression, they concluded that low self-control interacting with criminal opportunity predicted self-reported crimes of force and fraud.

These last steps, to a degree, follow the guidelines of developing the measurement of a construct set forth by psychometricians; the items were examined in a representative population using factor analysis. However, only EFA was completed in psychometrically testing this construct, not the more rigorous CFA. Furthermore, several items load poorly onto their respective factors (eight items with loadings less than 0.4, the standard cutoff), with one item removed

Table 1 Grasmick et al. 1993 measure of low self-control

Level of agreement on a four-point scale (4) strongly agree, (3) agree somewhat, (2) disagree somewhat, or (1) strongly disagree

Impulsivity

1. I often act on the spur of the moment without stopping to think.
2. I don't devote much thought and effort to preparing for the future.
3. I often do whatever brings me pleasure here and now, even at the cost of some distant goal.
4. I'm more concerned with what happens to me in the short run than in the long run.

Simple Tasks

5. I frequently try to avoid projects that I know will be difficult.
6. When things get complicated, I tend to quit or withdraw.
7. The things in life that are easiest to do bring me the most pleasure.
8. I dislike really hard tasks that stretch my abilities to the limit.

Risk Seeking

9. I like to test myself every now and then by doing something a little risky.
10. Sometimes I will take a risk just for the fun of it.
11. I sometimes find it exciting to do things for which I might get in trouble.
12. Excitement and adventure are more important to me than security.

Physical Activities

13. If I had a choice, I would almost always rather do something physical than something mental.
14. I almost always feel better when I am on the move than when I am sitting and thinking.
15. I like to get out and do things more than I like to read or contemplate ideas.
16. I seem to have more energy and a greater need for activity than most other people my age.*

Self-Centered

17. I try to look out for myself first, even if it means making things difficult for other people.
18. I'm not very sympathetic to other people when they are having problems.
19. If things I do upset people, it's their problem not mine.
20. I will try to get the things I want even when I know it's causing problems for other people.

Temper

21. I lose my temper pretty easily.
22. Often when I'm angry at people, I feel more like hurting them than talking to them about why I am angry.

Table 1 (cont.)

23. When I'm really angry, other people better stay away from me.
24. When I have a serious disagreement with someone, it's usually hard for me to talk calmly about it without getting upset.

* *Not included in later scales (and dropped from original analysis).*

from the analysis (Walker & Maddan, 2008). Additionally, the items and their responses were not evaluated using more advanced modern psychometric methods.

Since this scale's development, it has been used in a variety of samples and circumstances. For example, this scale has been used to examine associations of self-control with crime among university students in the United States and Japan (Kobayashi et al., 2010), cyber deviance among middle and high schoolers (Holt et al., 2012), and even morality and crime in adults in Ukraine (Antonacci & Tittle, 2008). In addition, components of this scale have been used to measure impulsivity (see, e.g., Becker, 2021; van Veen & Stattler, 2020) and risk-taking (see, e.g., Kim et al., 2012; Rebellon et al., 2019). This scale's wide use highlights the importance of the construct and is arguably a core construct of our field.

Grasmick et al. (1993) acknowledged the limits of their measure, encouraging "others to replicate our measure and develop other items" (p. 17). Notably, some researchers have taken up the challenge. For example, Piquero and colleagues (2000) were the first to use the modern psychometric measurement technique of IRT to address some of the issues with the measurement of self-control via Grasmick et al.'s scale. With a focus on the interaction between survey items and participants, they used IRT's Rasch model to test the influence of self-control on survey item response. Piquero and colleagues (2000) conclude that gender and individual self-control influenced the responses to survey items – they argued that the Grasmick et al. (1993) scale may be flawed.

Additionally, Higgins (2007) takes up the challenge, assessing the construct validity of the Grasmick et al. (1993) scale. Using a Rasch model, Higgins (2007) tests the original items from Grasmick et al. (1993) and reaches similar conclusions as Piquero et al. (2000) – the Grasmick et al. (1993) scale may be flawed. However, Higgins (2007) goes one step further and attempts to adjust Grasmick et al.'s self-control scale to improve it. After removing items that provided overfit or underfit and those that operated differentially for males and females, Higgins (2007) suggested a 16-item scale to measure self-control.

Beyond the Grasmick et al. Scale

Gottfredson and Hirschi's (1990) self-control theory has emerged as a dominant perspective within criminology. In this context, at issue is the development of the measurement of the concept of low self-control. Does Grasmick et al.'s (1993) scale remain influential? Have other measures emerged to rival this scale on methodological grounds? Most important, have any criminologists attempted to advance the measurement of self-control by using systematic psychometric methods from start to finish? The answer to this latter query appears to be no.

The results of our review of the measurement of low self-control are presented in Tables 2 and 3. The results are drawn from studies conducted in two periods: (1) those examined in Pratt and Cullen (2000), and (2) 11 studies published since 2023 in the field's top 20 "Criminology, Criminal Law & Policing" journals, based on Google Scholar. In Tables 2 and 3, we list whether studies relied on the Grasmick et al. scale and, if so, how many items they employed (as indicated by an X under each of the 24 items in the scale – see Table 2). If studies did not build on Grasmick et al., two sample items used to assess self-control are listed; the remaining items are in the Supplemental Materials.

First, the review of 21 manuscripts included in the Pratt and Cullen meta-analysis (see Table 2) illuminates the measurement of this construct up until 2000, using both primary and secondary data. Of the 13 studies that relied on primary data collection, 7 (of which one is Grasmick et al., 1993) used at least 9 items from Gramick et al.'s scale. Of the studies relying on secondary data, 5 used at least 8 of the 23 items. Studies that did not include Grasmick et al.'s scale (in full or part) used items that related (on their face) to Gottfredson and Hirschi's (1990) conceptualization of low self-control. Still, none of these scales were developed with contemporary psychometric methods.

Given that the Pratt and Cullen (2000) meta-analysis focused on the early studies of self-control, Table 3 reviews 11 contemporary studies. Were marked improvements in measuring self-control apparent? Tellingly, of the 3 studies that collected primary data, all used Grasmick et al.'s scale in part or full. That is, given the chance to develop their own (possibly psychometrically grounded) scale of self-control, these studies adopted the standard measure in the field – Grasmick et al. Of the studies relying on secondary data, only 2 of the 8 studies used at least three items from Grasmick et al. As with the secondary data studies of the previous era, alternative or additional items used to build a measure of self-control appear, on their face, to align with the conceptualization of this construct. However, none of these scales were derived using contemporary psychometric methods and analysis. Instead, for more than three decades,

Table 2 Low self-control measures from Pratt and Cullen meta-analysis

Article	Location	Type of Data	1	2	3	4	5	6	7	8	9	10	11	12	13	14	15	16	17	18	19	20	21	22	23	24	PD
Arneklev et al. (1993)	Large Southwestern city	Primary	X	X	X	X	X	X	X	X	X	X	X	X	X	X	X	X*	X	X	X	X	X	X	X	X	N
Burton et al. (1994)	Midwestern, urban area	Primary																									
• If someone insulted me, I would be likely to hit or slap them.																											N
• I like to take chances.																											
Burton et al. (1998) (see Burton et al. 1994)	Cincinnati, OH	Primary																									N
Burton et al. (1999) (see Burton et al. 1994)	Midwestern, urban area	Primary																									N
Cochran et al. (1996)	University of Oklahoma	Primary	?	?	?	?	?	?	?	?	?	?	?	?	?	?	?	?	?	?	?	?	?	?	?	?	N
Evans et al. (1997) (see Burton et al. 1994)	Midwestern, urban area	Primary																									N
Gibbs & Giever (1995)	Undergraduate liberal studies criminology course	Primary																									
• I get bored easily.																											N
• I like to take chances.																											
Gibbs et al. (1998)	Undergraduate liberal studies criminology course	Primary																									
• If it feels good, do it.					X								X	X	X					X	X	X	X		X			N
• I get mad pretty easily.																											

Table 2 (cont.)

Article	Location	Type of Data	1	2	3	4	5	6	7	8	9	10	11	12	13	14	15	16	17	18	19	20	21	22	23	24	PD
Grasmick et al. (1993)	Oklahoma City	Primary	X	X	X	X	X	X	X	X	X	X	X	X	X	X	X	X*	X	X	X	X	X	X	X	X	N
Nagin & Paternoster (1993)	University of Maryland	Primary	X	X	X	X	X	X	X	X	X	X	X	X	X	X	X	X	X	X	X	X	X	X	X	X	
Piquero & Tibbetts (1996)	Major East Coast University	Primary	X	X	X	X	X	X	X	X	X	X	X	X	X	X	X	X*	X	X	X	X	X	X	X	X	
Tremblay et al. (1995)	Montreal	Primary																									
• Gives up easily.																											
• Poor concentration or short attention span.																											
Wood et al. (1993)	Oklahoma	Primary																									
I don't devote much thought and effort to preparing for the future.				X	X	X	X	X	X	X	X	X	X	X	X	X	X	X	X	X	X	X	X	X	X	X	
Avakame (1998)	University of New Hampshire	Secondary																									
• Hostile or mean when drunk.																											N
• Frequently loses temper.																											
Brownfield & Sorenson (1993)	Richmond, VA	Secondary																									
• How much schooling do you actually expect to get eventually?																											N
• Overall, unweighted grade point average.																											
Longshore (1998)	Unknown	Secondary																									
• Careful.			X	X	X		X	X	X	X	X	X		X	X	X	X			X	X	X	X	X	X	X	N
Longshore & Turner (1998)	Unknown	Secondary																									
• Careful.			X	X	X		X	X	X	X	X	X		X	X	X	X			X	X	X	X	X	X	X	N

Longshore et al. (1996)	Unknown	Secondary																									
• Careful.			X	X	X		X	X	X	X	X	X		X	X	X	X			X	X	X	X	X	X	X	N
Piquero & Rosay (1998)	RAND – UCLA	Secondary																									
• Careful.			X	X	X		X	X	X	X	X	X		X	X	X	X			X	X	X	X	X	X	X	N
Polakowski (1994)	Great Britain	Secondary																									
• Risk/daring (mother/peer report).																											N
• Lacks concentration (teacher report).																											
• Grade achievements.																											
Winfree & Bernat (1998)	Phoenix, AZ & Las Cruces, NM	Secondary																									
• My parents know who I am with if I am not at home.			X	X	X	X					X	X	X	X													N
• My parents know where I am when I am not at school.																											

[*] PD = Psychometrically Developed.

Note: Scales using non-Grasmick et al. items provide two illustrative items, with full scales provided in the Supplemental Materials. Full manuscript reference information in the Supplemental Materials.

Table 3 Low self-control measures from 2023: Present top criminology and criminal justice journals

Article	Location	Type of Data	1	2	3	4	5	6	7	8	9	10	11	12	13	14	15	16	17	18	19	20	21	22	23	24	PD
Jang & Johnson (2024)	Dallas, TX	Primary	X								X								X				X				N
Pechorro et al. (2023)	University of Minho at Braga, Portugal	Primary	X	X	X	X	X	X	X	X	X	X	X	X	X	X	X		X	X	X	X	X	X	X	X	N
Smith et al. (2023)	Northeastern region of the United States	Primary	X	X	X	X	X	X	X	X	X	X	X	X	X	X	X	X	X	X	X	X	X	X	X	X	N
Brown et al. (2023)	Philadelphia, PA & Phoenix, AZ	Secondary																									UNK
• I do things without giving them much thought.																											
• People who make me angry better watch out.																											
Bryson et al. (2023)	South Korea	Secondary																									N
• I am apt to enjoy risky activities.																											
• I lose my temper whenever I get angry.																											
Kammigan (2023)	28 Countries	Secondary	X		X	X					X	X		X													N
Kim & Lee (2023) (none listed)	South Korea	Secondary																									N
Kim et al. (2023) (not listed)	South Korea	Secondary																									N

Meldrum et al. (2023)	Florida	Secondary	X		X			X	N
(3 items not listed)									
Ragan et al. (2023)	Pennsylvania & Iowa	Secondary							N
• Get information that is needed to deal with their problems.									
• Do what feels good, regardless of the consequences.									
TenEyck et al. (2023)	United States	Secondary							N
• Whether difficult problems made them upset.									
• Got along with their teachers.									

* PD = Psychometrically Developed.

Note: Scales using non-Grasmick et al. items provide two illustrative items, with full scales provided in the Supplemental Materials. Full manuscript reference information in the Supplemental Materials.

studies using this construct have largely relied on the original Grasmick et al. (1993) measure, which they acknowledge could use "further refinements in measurement" (p. 24). No criminologist has taken up the task of constructing a measure of low self-control using modern systematic psychometric methods. *This* is the hidden measurement crisis in criminology.

2.3.2 Measuring Collective Efficacy

With Robert Sampson as its main author, collective efficacy theory has emerged as the preeminent macrolevel theory of crime. The concept and its measurement were introduced in the iconic 1997 *Science* article that Sampson published with Stephen Raudenbush and Felton Earls, "Neighborhoods and Violent Crime: A Multilevel Study of Collective Efficacy." Sampson et al. (1997) capitalized on the unique nature of data from the Project on Human Development in Chicago Neighborhoods (PHDCN), whose large sample of 8,782 allowed them to aggregate respondents to form 343 "neighborhood clusters" (p. 919). This method enabled them to explore neighborhood effects and to use hierarchical linear modeling to control for "person-level predictors." The key question was: Which ecological variables, if any, would be associated with neighborhood rates of violence? The key finding was that collective efficacy's effects were robust across perceived violence, violent victimization, and homicide. This factor was negatively associated with all measures of violence and partially mediated the effects of structural factors, especially concentrated disadvantage.

The article not only reported stunning findings showing ecological effects but also introduced a new theoretical concept that offered a turning point in the systemic studies of communities: collective efficacy. Sampson et al. (1997) moved beyond social disorganization theory to a view of the modern metropolis where people interacted less but were capable of acting as a unit to solve troubling problems. What mattered was the ability of the *collective* to act in concert to *effectively* protect their values when threatened.

What remains hidden, however, is the real-life process used by Sampson et al. to construct their measure of collective efficacy. Building off his earlier work testing social disorganization directly (Sampson & Groves, 1989), Sampson played a role in designing the neighborhood measures of the PHDCN, including two key variables: "informal social control" and "social cohesion" (Sampson et al., 1997, pp. 919–920). Each scale was five items, which are listed in Table 4. As can be seen, the social cohesion items seem to have face validity, cohering around whether neighbors can be trusted and relied upon when needed.

By contrast, the informal social control items are a mixed bag. Items 1, 2, and 3 focus on the perceived willingness of neighbors to do something if children

Table 4 A measure of collective efficacy

Informal Social Control
Would you say it is very likely, likely, neither likely nor unlikely, unlikely, or very unlikely that your neighbors could be counted on to intervene in various ways:
1. Children were skipping school and hanging out on a street corner.
2. Children were spray-painting graffiti on a local building.
3. Children were showing disrespect to an adult.
4. A fight broke out in front of their house.
5. The fire station closest to their home was threatened with budget cuts.
Social Cohesion
Level of agreement on a five-point scale:
6. People around here are willing to help their neighbors.
7. This is a close-knit neighborhood.
8. People in this neighborhood can be trusted.
9. People in this neighborhood don't get along with each other (reverse coded).
10. People in this neighborhood do not share the same values (reverse coded).

misbehave. Item 4 asks about intervening if a fight broke out in front of their house. Notably, items 1–4 all call for a situational response, hardly time to organize the collective to act together to solve the problem. However, item 5 taps into this very possibility – whether residents would come together if the local fire station was threatened with budget cuts.

This measurement saga has one more chapter. When Sampson et al. (1997) checked for multicollinearity, they discovered that informal social control and social cohesion "were closely associated across neighborhoods (r = 0.80, $p <$ 0.001), which suggests that the two measures were tapping aspects of the same latent construct" (p. 920). What to do? The two scales could not be used separately as intended, but might they be merged? If so, would doing so make conceptual sense? Here is where Sampson et al.'s innovativeness once again surfaced:

> Because we also expected that the willingness and intention to intervene on behalf of the neighborhood would be enhanced under conditions of mutual trust and cohesion, we combined the two scales into a summary measure labeled collective efficacy. … [They offer] the image of local residents working collectively to solve their problems. (pp. 920, 923)

Sampson et al. realized that they were developing something new. Neighborhoods mattered not because they were urban villages with close family, kinship, and ethnic ties – the main thesis of the systemic model. Rather, they suggested that people could live mostly anonymously, driving into garages and staying in homes. However, if a problem arose that threatened community safety and shared values, could they organize to shut it down? If so, their actions would be an instance of collective efficacy.

In a clever analysis, Sampson et al. controlled for three variables that measured neighborhood organization/disorganization (see Sampson & Groves, 1989): "neighborhood services, friendship and kinship ties, and organizational participation" (Sampson et al., 1997, p. 922). In a supplemental analysis, they also controlled for "social interaction," such as had parties, watched each other's homes, and gave personal advice (p. 924, fn. 36). If collective efficacy continued to have strong independent effects on neighborhood violence, it would retain "discriminant validity." This was the case. Sampson et al. could argue that their novel concept was "theoretically relevant" (p. 923) and not confounded with social disorganization measures.

To be sure, Sampson et al. should be honored for conceptual innovation, for measuring their novel concept as best they could, and then for showing that their measure acted in a way consistent with their theoretical predictions. Sampson et al. (1997) provided researchers with a ready-made measure of collective efficacy for future research, which subsequent scholarship has built on their work productively. However, a critical assessment of their measure should have occurred many years ago. Our current critique is narrow, pertaining only to how collective efficacy was measured. It fully recognizes Sampson and his colleagues' contribution in offering the theoretically powerful concept of collective efficacy and empirically compelling analyses.

First, it is obvious that Sampson et al. (1997) did not develop a measure of collective efficacy using systematic modern psychometric methods. Because the concept of collective efficacy was invented *after* the informal social control and social cohesion items were decided upon and the data collected, it was impossible to create a pool of possible items/indicators and whittle them down.

Second, although the scale items are suggestive, only the fire station item directly assesses *collective efficacy* – "of local residents working collectively to solve their problems" (Sampson et al., 1997, p. 923). The informal social control items focus on situational misconduct that would most often require a rapid *individual* response by a resident (e.g., call the police to stop a fight). The events described in these items could lead to a collective response, but such action is not measured directly. The items do not focus on how neighbors would *come together* to solve a problem (e.g., neighborhood watch). The items were not developed to measure collective efficacy; they were appropriated for that purpose, providing limited face and content validity.

This assessment offers a critical analysis of Sampson et al. (1997), but it would be reductionistic not to applaud their creativity, theoretical brilliance, and quantitative rigor. They transformed the field of macrolevel criminology and produced a classic work in the process. Rather, this discussion is meant more as a criticism of the rest of us, who typically have used their measure of collective efficacy without comment and made no effort to improve their scale through psychometric methods. Let us hasten to add that Sampson et al.'s scale could have strong psychometric properties. However, without criminometrics to study this possibility, speculation only exists. We develop this point more broadly in Section 5.

Our content analysis supports this conclusion. Using studies published since 2019 in the top 20 "Criminology, Criminal Law & Policing" journals, based on Google Scholar, our search yielded 19 quantitative studies using collective efficacy as a variable.[1] Table 5 shows that 8 studies conducted primary data collection and the remaining 11 relied upon secondary data analysis. Distinguishing between primary and secondary data analysis provides us the opportunity to reflect on whether criminologists have attempted to improve upon Samson et al.'s scale, given the opportunity to do so (i.e., primary data collection) or have attempted to use other measures/proxies for this construct (i.e., secondary data analysis).

Across the eight studies engaged in primary data collection, every single one used at least three items from the Sampson et al. scale. Additionally, six of the eight added other items to their measure of collective efficacy (e.g., a group of kids was climbing on a parked car). Across the eleven secondary data studies, eight used at least one of Sampson et al.'s items, and four used the entirety of Sampson et al.'s scale. Three other studies supplemented Sampson et al.'s scale with additional items (e.g., Many of my neighbors know me.). Ultimately, none of the analyzed scales of this construct were developed using a fully developed psychometric approach. Criminologists have had more than 25 years to undertake this task but have not done so.

Where does this leave us? Clearly, Sampson et al.'s measure captures an important social reality related to crime across contexts. But precisely what it is measuring remains suggestive. As intimated, a critical research opportunity now presents itself: An investigation that develops a systematic measure of collective efficacy should be undertaken. These results can be used both to assess the original measure of collective efficacy and to potentially employ the new and improved measure in a fresh round of investigations.

[1] Searched scholarly databases (EBSCO HOST, 2021–2024, CJ Abstracts w/ full text, Academic Search Complete, Sociological Collection, Psychology and Behavioral Sciences Collection) with the search terms "collective efficacy criminology," on March 30, 2024.

Table 5 Collective efficacy measures

Article	Location	Type of Data	1	2	3	4	5	6	7	8	9	10	PD
Ferretti et al. (2019)	Italy	Primary	X	X	X	X	X	X	X	X	X	X	N
Hardyns et al. (2019)	Ghent, Belgium	Primary	X	X	X			X	X	X	X		N
• Children were making too much racket.													
• Children are using soft drugs (smoking weed, hash, etc.).													
Hardyns et al. (2023)	Ghent, Belgium	Primary	X	X	X			X	X	X	X		N
• Children were making too much racket.													
• Children are using soft drugs (smoking weed, hash, etc.).													
Jing et al. (2021)	Guangzhou, China	Primary						X	X		X		N
• Visiting informally with neighbors.													
• Chatting with neighbors.													
Kuen et al. (2022)	Baltimore, MD	Primary	X	X	X	X	X	X	X	X	X	X	N
• A group of kids was climbing on a parked car.													
• Neighbors watch out for each other on your block.													
Weisburd et al. (2021)	Brooklyn Park, Minnesota	Primary						X	X	X	X		N

• A group of kids was climbing on a parked car. • The local community center was going to be closed down because of budget cuts.													
Weisburd et al. (2020)	Baltimore, MD	Primary	X		X	X	X	X	X	X	X	X	N
• Neighbors do NOT talk to each other on your block. • Neighbors watch out for each other on your block.													
Wu & Liu (2023)	Southeast city in China	Primary	X	X	X	X	X	X	X	X			N
Chouhy & Unnever (2022)	Chicago, IL	Secondary	X	X	X	X	X	X	X	X	X	X	N
Danielsson (2021)	Finland	Secondary	X	X	X	X	X	X	X	X	X		N
• Drunken people were disturbing other residents. • There were loud noises coming from an apartment during the night.													
Dulin (2022)	Mexico	Secondary											N
• Whether or not the majority of residents in the neighborhood organized to resolve the problem (robberies and gangs).													
Farren (2023)	Eight European countries	Secondary	X	X	X	X							N

Table 5 (cont.)

Article	Location	Type of Data	1	2	3	4	5	6	7	8	9	10	PD
• Many of my neighbors know me. • People in my neighborhood often do things together.													
Gearhart & Tucker (2020)	United States	Secondary	?	X	?	X	?	X	X	?	?	?	N
Lanfear (2022)	Chicago, IL	Secondary	X	X	X	X	X	X	X	X	X	X	N
Lymperopoulou et al. (2022)	Greater Manchester (UK)	Secondary											N
• [Density of charities]													
O'Brien et al. (2021)	Boston, MA	Secondary	X	X	X	X	X	X	X	X	X	X	N
Stults & Swagar (2021)	Chicago, IL	Secondary	X	X	X	X	X	X	X	X	X	X	N
Thomson (2021)	799 southern counties	Secondary											N
• [Black Protestant affiliation rate]													
Yesberg et al. (2023)	London	Secondary			X								N
• Local people and authorities have control over the public space in this area. • If I sensed trouble whilst in this area, I could get help from people who live here.													

* PD = Psychometrically Developed.

Note: Scales using non-Sampson et al. items provide two illustrative items, with full scales provided in the Supplemental Materials. Full manuscript reference information in the Supplemental Materials.

2.4 Conclusion

This section had two purposes. First, we reviewed the steps involved in a modern psychometric approach to developing a measure of a concept. Second, we showed that criminologists do not use this modern systematic psychometric approach when creating new conceptual measures. In fact, once a prominent measure is constructed and published, it is often accepted and used repeatedly without question. Such measures can persist for decades with limited efforts to improve their measurement properties. That is the crisis we seek to unmask. A revolution in criminometrics is needed. As the sections ahead reveal, it is possible to develop criminological concepts using systematic psychometric methods. Doing so is challenging, but the benefits may be untold.

3 The Concept of Procedural Justice

To provide an example of how the field might address this measurement crisis, we focus on *procedural justice*, a major construct informing theory, research, and practice in policing. Procedural justice has been investigated extensively, producing numerous studies and a large volume of literature. In this context, we selected this construct for our case study because of its lengthy tenure as a construct, its noted heterogeneous measurement and operationalization (Mazerolle, Bennett, et al., 2013, p. 257), and its importance for police–community relations (President's Task Force on 21st Century Policing, 2015).

In this section, we take on the first step for building a measure of a construct set forth by the American Educational Research Association (AERA) et al. (2014) – defining and conceptualizing the construct using theory. We begin by situating the concept of procedural justice and its measurement within the policing literature before we move to the construct's theoretical origins and extensions. Finally, we turn to the challenges in measuring procedural justice.

3.1 Procedural Justice and Police Reform

Over the past few decades, policing in the United States has engaged in a sustained reform movement (Weisburd & Braga, 2006; President's Task Force on 21st Century Policing, 2015). Calls have been made to curtail the adverse outcomes of police–citizen interactions through reforms such as implementing citizen review boards, requiring officers to wear body cameras, and providing implicit bias and de-escalation training to police (see, e.g., Engel et al., 2020; Graham, McManus, et al., 2019; Ivkovic, 2014; Nix et al., 2017; Worden et al., 2020). Most relevant to our concerns, another prominent reform has been to have police officers engage with the community using "procedures" that are perceived as fair. Thus, the first "organizing pillar" advanced by the Obama administration's President's Task Force on 21st Century Policing (2015, p. 11) was "Building Trust and Legitimacy"; Recommendation 1.1 was to "adopt procedural justice as the guiding principle for internal and external policies and practices to guide [police] interactions with the citizens they serve."

This use of "procedural justice" – defined as "the nature of the process governing dispute resolutions" (Tyler & Folger, 1980, p. 281) – builds on the work of Tom Tyler and others, who found that community members' evaluation of a police encounter hinged not just on the outcome (e.g., arrested or not) but also on their treatment during the interaction (Mazerolle, Bennett, et al., 2013; Sunshine & Tyler, 2003a; Tyler, 1990, 2004, 2017; Tyler & Folger, 1980; Tyler & Huo, 2002). Tyler (2000) emphasized that, among other potential influences, citizens responded more favorably, regardless of the outcome of the contact, when they (1) were provided with an opportunity to express their voice, (2) were treated with dignity and respect, (3) perceived the officer as neutral, and (4) believed the officer to have trustworthy motives.

Regardless of how procedural justice was defined, conceptualized, or measured, voluminous research has assessed the impact of procedural justice in policing. Studies have examined outcomes such as satisfaction with police (Mastrofski et al., 2016; Mazerolle et al., 2015; Mazerolle et al., 2012; Murphy et al., 2008; Tyler & Folger, 1980; Tyler & Huo, 2002), cooperation with police (Bolger & Walters, 2019; Graham, Kulig, et al. 2019; Mazerolle et al., 2015; Mazerolle et al., 2012; Murphy et al., 2022; Sunshine & Tyler, 2003a, 2003b; Tyler, 1990, 2004; Tyler & Huo, 2002; Van Damme, 2013; Van Damme et al., 2015), legitimacy (Eckert, 2009; Gau, 2015; MacQueen & Bradford, 2015; Mazerolle, Antrobus, et al., 2013; Murphy et al., 2008; Murray et al., 2021; Weisburd et al., 2022), trust (Madon et al., 2023; Murphy, 2023; Nägel & Nivette, 2023; Sahin et al., 2024), confidence and trust (Sahin et al., 2017), cooperation and trust (Nalla & Nam, 2021), recidivism (Van Hall et al., 2023), and compliance (Dai, 2007; Murphy, 2009, 2023; Murphy et al., 2008; Murry et al., 2021; Sunshine & Tyler, 2003a, 2003b; Tyler, 1990).

These works provide important insights into the merits of procedural justice. Time and again, however, scholars attempting to understand this body of knowledge run into a common roadblock – the measures used to assess procedural justice are so diverse that these studies cannot be coherently summarized (Gau, 2011, 2014; Graham, Pratt, et al., 2020; Harkin, 2015; Johnson et al., 2014; Maguire & Johnson, 2010; Mazerolle, Bennett, et al., 2013; Reisig et al., 2007). In their meta-analysis of this literature, Mazerolle, Bennett, and colleagues (2013) note that there was "substantial heterogeneity among conceptual and operational definitions of key outcomes," including procedural justice, which limited their ability to reach definitive conclusions about these outcomes (p. 257). Gau (2011, 2014) has also taken issue with the measurement of procedural justice, stating that "the time has come for the measurement of procedural justice and police legitimacy to receive direct, full attention by researchers in this field" (2014, p. 204).

Therefore, the current Element takes up this challenge to develop a measure of procedural justice for policing. As an important first step, we start by tracing the roots of procedural justice. That is, where did this construct come from, how was it originally envisioned, how has the construct changed (conceptually and operationally) over time, and where are we now?

3.2 Origins of Procedural Justice

Although the implementation of practices designed to increase procedural justice is a prominent policing reform, the theoretical origins of the idea extend to the writings of legal and social psychology scholars in the 1970s and 1980s. Focusing on the courtroom setting, researchers sought to illuminate the mechanisms and impact of fair procedures in dispute resolution. Most prominently, Thibaut and Walker (1975, 1978) argued that it was not merely the outcome of a courtroom dispute that was important; the process for how the decisions were reached also played a role in perceptions of fairness. They conducted several experiments testing this proposition, finding that the fairness of procedures plays an important role in both parties being satisfied with an outcome, favorable or otherwise. These procedures included satisfaction that all evidence was presented and that the opportunity for both sides to present evidence was just, and a sense that the overall procedure was fair to all parties involved in the dispute.

A parallel line of research by Leventhal (1980) approached procedural justice through a theoretical lens, focusing on perceived inadequacies of sociology's equity theory and presenting his own "justice judgment model" (Figure 1). In short, his model presumed that judgments of fairness were based on several justice rules, which can be categorized into distributional or procedural. He also proposed that individuals hold an internal "cognitive map" that contains information about the structural features of an allocative process, which would inform the applicable procedural rules. To arrive at a decision about whether a process was fair or not, Leventhal (1980) proposed that an individual identifies and provides weights to the relevant rules in a given situation before developing a preliminary estimation of a "fair" outcome based on each of these rules and their weights. The individual then combines the total of these estimations before assessing fairness.

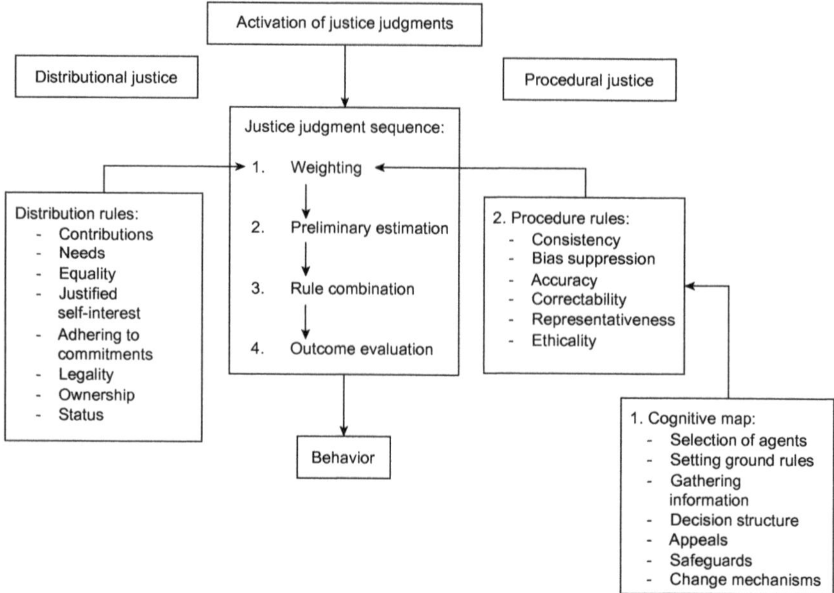

Figure 1 Leventhal's (1980) justice judgment model.

Albeit both Thibaut and Walker (1975, 1978) and Leventhal (1980) likely contributed in parallel veins to the foundation of procedural justice, Thibaut and Walker (1975, 1978) are largely credited with the first theory of just procedures. Still, they did not provide an explicit list of items to measure procedural justice, nor did they describe the core components of procedural justice. In contrast, Leventhal (1980) set forth a clear definition of procedural justice: "an individual's perception of the fairness of procedural components of the social system that regulate the allocative process" which furthermore "focuses on the individual's cognitive map of events that precede the distribution of reward, and the evaluation of those events" (p. 35).

Leventhal (1980) also outlines a preliminary set of components (i.e., cognitive map) that may be judged by a set of six procedural rules. Both spent time conceptualizing and attempting to measure procedural justice, as is recommended by the AERA et al. (2014). Nonetheless, it is the work of Thibaut and Walker that would prove influential to criminology and criminal justice.

3.3 Extensions of Procedural Justice

Building on this work of Thibaut and Walker (1975), Tyler and Folger (1980) applied the concept of procedural justice to a less formal legal interaction – police–community contacts. To test whether these interactions had a procedural

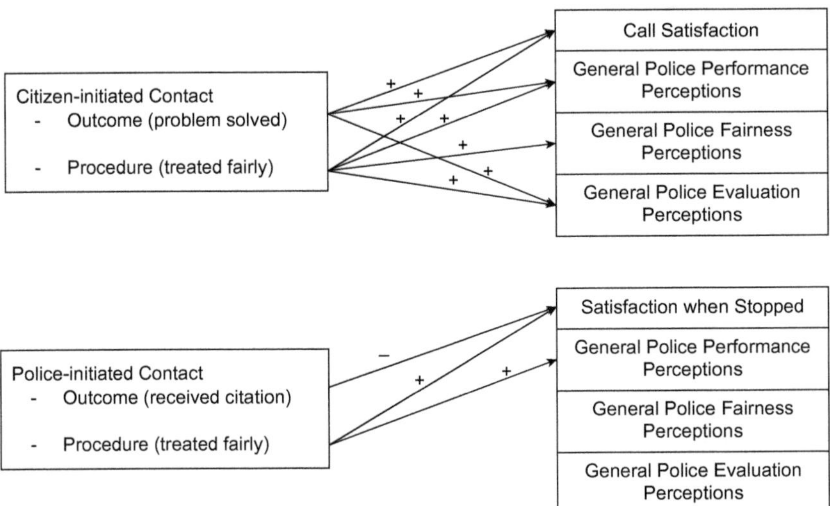

Figure 2 Tyler and Folger (1980): The influence of procedural justice on specific satisfaction and general perceptions of police.

component, Tyler and Folger (1980) surveyed 184 Evanston, Illinois, residents. As seen in Figure 2, in both citizen- and police-initiated contacts, perceptions about the officer "treating the respondent fairly" and the outcome of the contact significantly influenced the respondent's satisfaction with the police (p. 285). However, in the context of police-initiated contacts, the perceived fair treatment by the officer was more important than the outcome of the contact (i.e., receiving a citation) when determining satisfaction with the contact.

Continuing from this early work, Tyler's (1990) pioneering book *Why People Obey the Law* situated procedural justice in the context of police legitimacy and compliance with the legal statutes. In seeking to discern the antecedents of obedience, Tyler (1990) examined not only perceptions of legitimacy but also procedural justice, distributive justice, effectiveness, the performance of authorities, personal morality, and deterrence. After identifying procedural justice as a key antecedent of legitimacy, he turned to identifying the core criteria used to judge the fairness of a procedure (i.e., how to measure procedural justice).

Drawing on Leventhal (1980) as well as Thibaut and Walker (1975, 1978), as seen in Figure 3, Tyler examined seven elements in the context of policing and the courts: process control, decision control, consistency (toward people and over time), impartiality, accuracy/quality of decisions, correctability, and ethicality. To evaluate their independent contribution to perceptions of fairness, Tyler used these elements as predictors to explain variation in responses to "how fair the procedures used by the police or courts were and how fairly the respondents

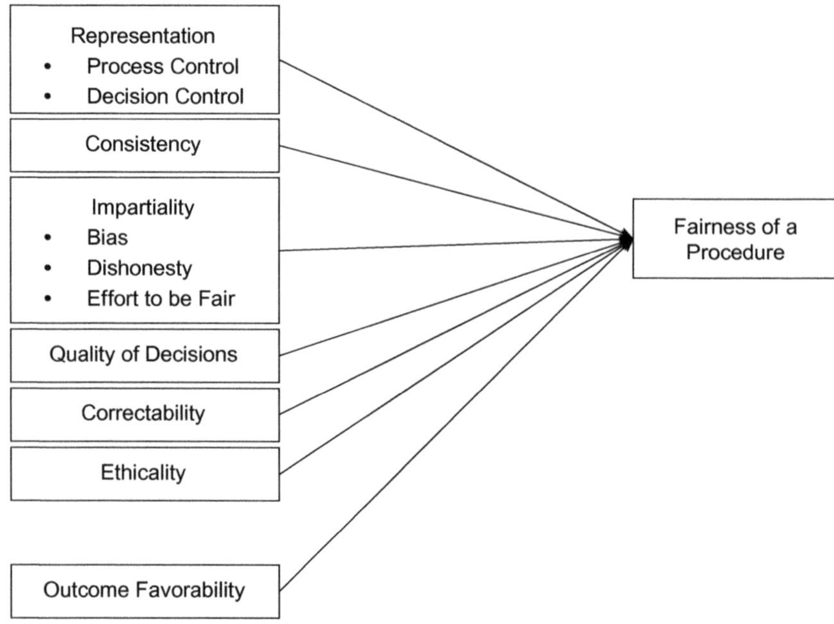

Figure 3 Tyler's (1990) theoretical model of criteria used to judge fairness of a procedure.

were treated" in their experience (Tyler, 1990, p. 92). As seen in Figure 4, even after accounting for the favorability of the outcome, six things exerted significant influence on the fairness of the procedures used by the police and courts: views about whether the authorities (1) tried to be fair, (2) were dishonest with community members, (3) were ethical, (4) provided representation, and (5) provided quality decision-making. Furthermore, factor analyses by Tyler (1990) demonstrated a potential for dimensionality in the measure of procedural justice. The first factor was composed of consistency, politeness, and concern for rights. The second factor was composed of whether authorities made an effort to be fair and to solve the problem, and the quality of their decisions.

Throughout the next decade of work, Tyler's views about the antecedents of obedience and procedural justice evolved, as did the measurement of these constructs. Under the group value model (Lind & Tyler, 1988), Tyler (1989) grouped his previously used seven elements (which are listed within parentheses) into four categories. These included (1) control (process control and decision control); (2) neutrality (consistency toward people and over time, impartiality, accuracy/quality of decision-making) (3) trust (impartiality); and (4) standing (ethicality). Again, he found that, even after controlling for a host of potential confounds, the variables of control, neutrality, trust, and standing

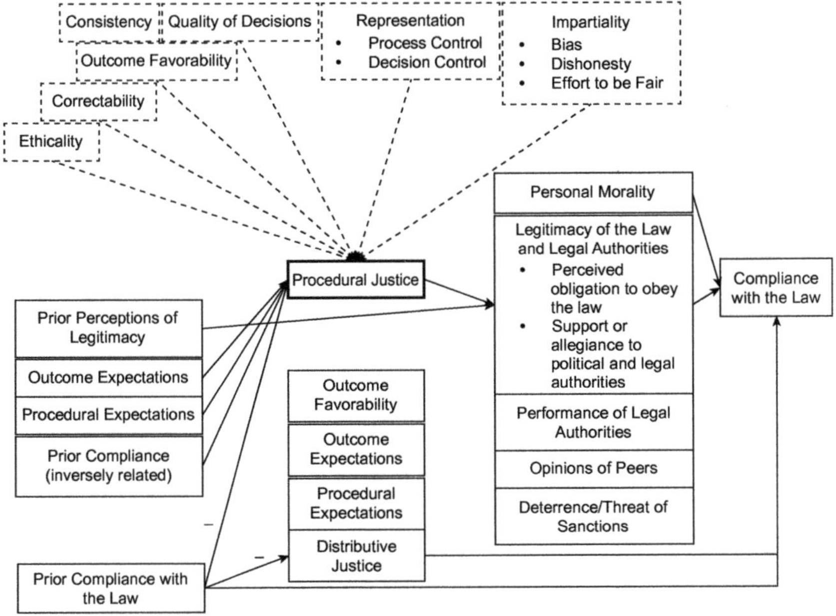

Figure 4 Summary of Tyler's (1990) findings.

each had independent and significant effects in viewing a procedure as fair. Under their relational model of authority (Figure 5), Tyler and Lind (1992) similarly conceptualized procedural justice as trust (concern for needs, consideration of views), standing (dignity/politeness, respect for rights), and neutrality (absence of bias/prejudice, honesty, fact-based decision-making).

Several years later, after recognizing the seemingly limitless elements that influence procedural justice, Tyler and Blader (2000) proposed a two-component and four-component model defining procedural justice. The purpose of these reconceptualizations was to "consolidate constructs and ideas that may have the same theoretical underpinnings" (Tyler & Blader, 2000, p. 106). Under the two-component model, elements that influenced views of procedural fairness were grouped into (1) "quality of decision-making process" (e.g., decisions are made based upon facts, not personal biases and opinions; the rules and procedures are equally fair to everyone) and (2) "quality of treatment" (e.g., my rights are respected when decisions are made; my views are considered when decisions are made) (Tyler & Blader, 2000, pp. 103–104). Under the four-component model, these elements are grouped by the source (i.e., formal, informal) of the procedural justice judgment and the content (e.g., quality of decision-making, quality of treatment). As seen in Figure 6, this approach yielded four categories: (1) formal quality of decision-making,

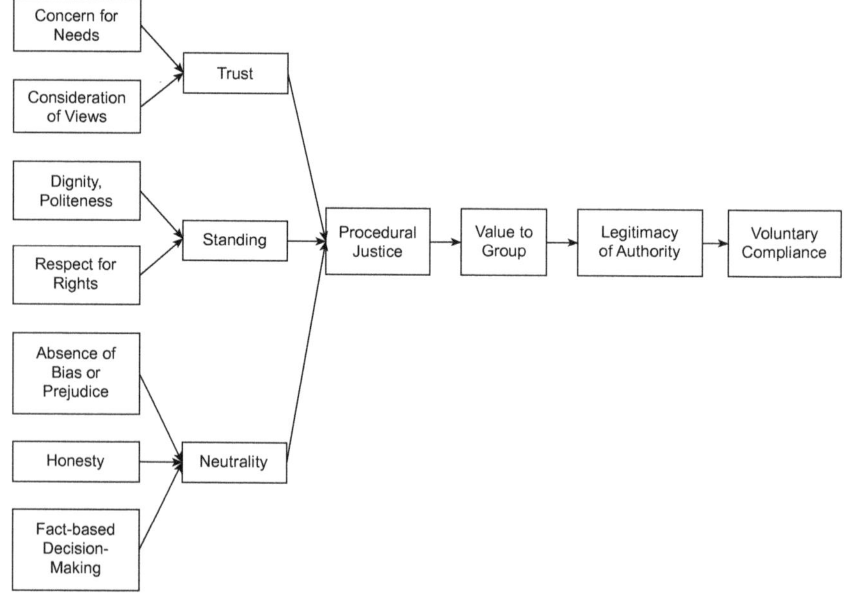

Figure 5 Tyler and Lind's (1992) relational model of authority.

		Source	
		Formal	Informal
Procedural Element	Quality of decision-making processes	Formal quality of decision-making	Informal quality of decision-making
	Quality of treatment	Formal quality of treatment	Informal quality of treatment

*From Tyler and Blader (2000, p. 12)

Figure 6 Tyler and Blader's (2000) four components of procedural justice.*

(2) informal quality of decision-making, (3) formal quality of treatment, and (4) informal quality of treatment (Tyler & Blader, 2000). Analyses of the two-component and four-component arrangements produced viable models for categorizing elements. As such, these reconceptualizations of procedural justice point to a broader issue for scholars: Researchers must attend to conceptual developments and changes in a construct to ensure measurement of a construct reflects these changes.

Notably, Tyler (2000) attempted to synthesize the social justice literature across several domains (e.g., courts, police, organizational psychology).

Although not a systematic review or meta-analysis, Tyler (2000) provides an overarching framework, concluding that four main elements primarily contribute to the perceptions of fair procedures (i.e., procedural justice). First, termed "voice," "participation," or "process control," the ability to participate in the decision-making process contributes to perceptions of fairness by providing an opportunity to discuss the contexts of a conflict, even if it does not change the outcome. Second, Tyler (2000) notes the importance of the perceived neutrality of authorities – that is, the belief that authorities are objective and impartial in the rules they follow and the decisions they make, not allowing personal biases or values to impact decisions. Third, the motives of the authority are integral to assessing procedural justice – also referred to as "trustworthiness."[2] Here, people are concerned with whether authorities are "benevolent and caring, [are] concerned about their situation and their concerns and needs, consider their arguments, [try] to do what is right for them, and [try] to be fair" (Tyler, 2000, p. 122). Fourth, being treated with dignity and respect by authorities implicitly tells people that authorities recognize their dignity of and their status as members of society. It is these four key elements that Tyler (2000) identifies as foundational to perceptions of procedural justice across any given situation.

Beyond his four elements, Tyler (2000) notes that several more elements might influence perceptions of procedural fairness depending on the situation and its contexts. He cautions that several studies find eight or more elements (e.g., perceived honesty of authorities; Tyler, 1988), including these four, might influence these perceptions, depending on the decision-making processing being studied. Thus, conceptually, researchers studying procedural justice should not only include these four elements but also seek to discern other elements that might impact perceptions of procedural justice and that might be unique to the decision-making process being studied. That is, concerning content validity, any measure of procedural justice in policing needs to conceptually contain these four elements and potentially other elements.

3.4 Challenges of Measuring Procedural Justice

The challenge for researchers is how best to conceptualize and measure procedural justice. Although the items used by many scholars to assess the concept have face validity, there is no agreed-upon measure, let alone conceptualization.

2 Trustworthiness should be considered distinct from "trust" (i.e., trust in the institution of policing, e.g., Jackson & Bradford, 2010; Sunshine & Tyler, 2003a). For more, see Mazerolle, Bennett, et al. (2013).

Should researchers conceptualize procedural justice using Tyler's (2000) four elements (i.e., trust, neutrality, voice, dignity/respect), his (1990) seven elements (i.e., process control, decision control, consistency, quality of decisions, impartiality, correctability, ethicality), his (Tyler & Blader, 2000) two-component model (i.e., quality of decision-making, quality of treatment), his (Tyler & Blader, 2000) four-component model (i.e., formal quality of decision-making, formal quality of treatment, informal quality of decision-making, informal quality of treatment), "subjective" or "objective" procedural justice (Trinkner, 2023; Worden & McLean, 2017), or something else entirely? Policing scholars have yet to decide.

Furthermore, how many and which items should be used to best capture these elements or components? Whether adopted items are included in secondary data sets or created anew in primary data sets, key elements of procedural justice, as identified by Tyler (2000; i.e., voice, neutrality, trustworthiness, dignity/respect), are measured differently or absent in the literature concerning procedural justice. For example, in the context of policing, in one study, voice is measured through agreement to the following statements: "Police gave me a chance to express my views before making decisions," "police considered my views," "police tried to take account of my needs," and "police cared about my concerns" (Elliott et al., 2011). However, in another, voice was measured through agreement to "the police in this area deal with things that matter to people," and "the police in this area listen to the concerns of local people" (Singer, 2013).

This pattern repeats with Tyler's element of trustworthiness – "the police make decisions to handle problems fairly," "the police can be trusted to make decisions that are right for your community," "the police follow through on their decisions and promises they make," and "the police make decisions based on the facts" (Czapska et al., 2014) versus "I felt the police were trustworthy," and "I had confidence the police were doing the right thing" (Bates et al., 2016).

These examples illustrate substantial heterogeneity in the number and wording of items used to measure procedural justice in policing. This is not to say that the items just listed or those found in extant scales are wrong. However, without a systematic approach to the conceptualization and operationalization of a measure of procedural justice, the collation of knowledge about procedural justice is limited (see Gau, 2011, 2014; Mazerolle, Bennet, et al., 2013).

3.5 Moving Forward

Given this backdrop, constructing a measure of procedural justice with modern psychometric methods is a worthy endeavor, with the potential to serve not only as a tool for policing scholars but also as a case study for criminology more broadly. As will be demonstrated in the coming sections, building any measure of a construct is a daunting task, but the benefits are plentiful. In Section 4, we begin with a robust pool of items, progressively whittling them down to a final measure of procedural justice. We will then adjudicate the value of this measure by comparing it to other measures, illustrating the need for a criminometric approach to measuring *all* criminological constructs.

4 Measuring Procedural Justice

Thus far, we have demonstrated the importance of procedural justice in policing and its measurement challenges. This section of the Element takes on the task of constructing a measure of procedural justice for policing using modern psychometric methods. Following a systematic review of items used to measure procedural justice and policing, we present a series of four surveys and modern psychometric methods to reduce a pool of 124 items to 10 of the best items that, taken together, should be used to measure this construct. More broadly, this section provides a road map for those who wish to measure other criminological constructs psychometrically – that is, to engage in criminometrics.

Providing this "case study" involves three sections. First, we outline the methods – that is, the "steps" taken to define our construct, develop a broad pool of items, pilot these items using a survey, and through an iterative process (of three surveys), remove poorly performing items from this pool using contemporary psychometric analysis – as is recommended by the AERA et al. (2014). All this allows us to arrive at and validate our recommended 10-item scale for procedural justice in policing. A fourth survey – a national-level survey fielded by YouGov – is used in this process. Second, the analytical strategy used in psychometrically assessing the quality of each item in our surveys is described. Third, the results of the analysis are presented for each survey. The goal is for this process to yield a measure of procedural justice based on modern psychometric methods, which can be adopted by the field for use across multiple studies, thus providing a firm and consistent foundation for us to build scientific knowledge about the impact of procedural justice in policing.

As a prelude to this case study, it is useful to review the distinction between CTT – a common approach used to assess the validity and reliability of criminological constructs at the test/scale level – and IRT – a more advanced psychometric method, which assesses the reliability and validity of a measure at the test/scale level *and* the item level. However, this review is not intended to provide a complete in-depth understanding of IRT (for more, see, e.g., de Ayala, 2009).

4.1 Classical Test Theory (CTT) versus Item Response Theory (IRT)

Both CTT and IRT are psychometric approaches used to evaluate the reliability and validity of tests/scales. Criminologists are likely quite familiar with the older CTT (also known as true score theory), which attempts to model latent traits using multiple items or questions (de Ayala, 2009; Hambleton & Jones, 1993). Analyses and statistics in this paradigm include EFA, CFA, item factor loadings, and Cronbach's α. Upon meeting or exceeding accepted cutoffs in these aforementioned statistics, items are combined (often summed or averaged) to produce a measure/score of the latent trait.

Within the CTT paradigm, a few assumptions exist that have important implications (for a summary, see Table 6). First, it assumes that any latent trait being

Table 6 Main differences between classical and item response theories and models*

Area	Classical test theory	Item response theory
Model	Linear	Nonlinear
Level	Test	Item
Assumptions	Weak (i.e., easy to meet with test data)	Strong (i.e., more difficult to meet with test data)
Item–ability relationship	Not specified	Item characteristic functions
Ability	Test scores or estimated true scores are reported on the test score scale (or a transformed test score scale)	Ability scores are reported on the scale of $-\infty$ to $+\infty$ (or a transformed scale)
Invariance of item and person statistics	No – item and person parameters are sample dependent	Yes – item and person parameters are sample independent, if model fits the test data
Item statistics	*p, r*	B, a, and c (for the three-parameter model) plus corresponding item information functions
Sample size (for item parameter estimation)	200 to 500 (in general)	Depends on the IRT model but larger samples, i.e., over 500, in general, are needed

* From Hambleton & Jones (1993).

measured is an "observed score," which is composed of a "true score" plus "random error" (Hambleton & Jones, 1993). If there were no "error" in measuring the latent trait, we could obtain the "true score"; however, this is not possible. As such, researchers aim to minimize this error as much as possible. A second assumption of CTT is that the latent trait increases monotonically, assuming items used to measure the latent trait are coded so that higher scores indicate more of the latent trait (Hambleton & Jones, 1993). Third, it is assumed in CTT that errors are normally distributed, are uncorrelated with parallel tests, and are uncorrelated with the "true score" of the latent trait (Hambleton & Jones, 1993). Analyses within this paradigm assume that items are measured continuously, absent of outliers, correlated, and linear, and that the latent trait is continuous and unidimensional (Flora et al., 2012; Hambleton & Jones, 1993; Watkins, 2018). Violations of these assumptions influence the accuracy of these analyses (Flora et al., 2012).

In contrast, IRT, which also seeks to model a continuous latent trait using multiple items, is an advance in psychometric methods because it focuses on the item level (see summary in Table 6). Item response theory has several features. First, it assesses an item's (and test's) performance in relation to the latent trait being measured (Hambleton & Jones, 1993). As such, items and respondents are placed on the same unidimensional continuum of the latent trait (mean of zero, standard deviation of one), which allows for the assessment of items and their ability to differentiate – also known as discrimination – between individuals along this continuum (de Ayala, 2009).

Second, using IRT also allows for modeling items with differing difficulty (or ease) of endorsement (de Ayala, 2009). A measure of entirely "easy" items may prove less informative than one with a mix of "easy" and "difficult" items (Nunnally & Bernstein, 1978). Therefore, the strengths and weaknesses of individual items within a scale can be vetted (de Ayala, 2009; Hambleton & Jones, 1993). Third, within the IRT framework, predictions about responses can be estimated by knowing the difficulty of an item (de Ayala, 2009; Hambleton & Jones, 1993; Hambleton et al., 1991). Fourth, because IRT is not sample-dependent (unlike CTT), once constructed and validated, items and scales can be used to estimate the latent trait of individuals outside of the original samples (Hambleton & Jones, 1993). Likewise, knowing the latent trait of a specific subpopulation, a specialized test/measure can be constructed using the known statistical parameters of specific items (Hambleton & Jones, 1993).

A strength of IRT is that items used to measure a latent trait can be continuously or categorically measured, with ordered or unordered categories (de Ayala, 2009; Hambleton & Jones, 1993). However, it has more rigorous assumptions than CTT, depending on the IRT model (e.g., Rasch models, one-parameter logistic models, two-parameter logistic models; Hambleton & Jones,

1993; for more detail on IRT methods, see de Ayala, 2009). Furthermore, IRT analyses generally require a larger sample size than CTT analyses. Finally, IRT analyses provide for the construction of response patterns or ability scores, which allow for the use of all item response information in later analysis, or as summed or averaged scales (as is done in CTT; Hambleton & Jones, 1993; Thissen et al., 1995).

Along with IRT's ability to examine item-level traits, IRT also provides for the assessment of a test's (or scale's) traits in order to assess the reliability of a set of items across the continuum of the underlying trait – that is, the "test information function" (TIF) (Hambleton & Jones, 1993). Visually plotted curves of a test's information function explain the reliability of the test across the continuum of the latent trait (Hambleton & Jones, 1993). A similar visual, known as the item information curve (IIF), can provide insight into which items are contributing information (or reliability) and where across the continuum of the latent trait (Hambleton & Jones, 1993). Thus items that contribute little additional information along (or at a specific point) the continuum might be removed from a test or scale to aid in producing a shorter test or scale (Hambleton et al., 1991). Ultimately, given the strengths of IRT to assess item difficulty and discrimination as well as test reliability across the continuum of latent traits, we will engage with both CTT and IRT throughout the analyses.

4.2 Methods

The process used to construct a measure of procedural justice involved *five steps*. As described, Step 1 of this process was to define the construct, delineating its boundaries and distinctions from related constructs. Based on Section 3, in this Element, we adopt the following definition: "the perception of fairness of the procedures and processes used by police or law enforcement officers from the perspective of community members." In contrast to related constructs, such as police legitimacy and satisfaction, this definition focuses on the processes police employ to reach decisions, specifically views of in/equity arising from these procedures. Alternatively, police legitimacy focuses on the acknowledgment that the police rightfully wield authority (Tyler, 1990, 2004), and satisfaction with police is a more global measure of positive emotions about police performance (see, e.g., Frank et al., 1996).

Given this definition, Step 2 requires the development of a pool of items from which to construct a measure. Because of the vast use of procedural justice in studying policing over the past 20 years, a systematic search and review of these studies was completed to extract the myriad of ways previous researchers have measured this concept. Following the recommendations of Chandler and colleagues

(2017) regarding systematic searches, specific criteria were set forth prior to the search regarding the selection of databases,[3] the selection of keywords,[4] and the timeframe of the search.[5] Studies were limited to those that attempted to measure procedural justice in policing using empirical means, and the search excluded studies that strictly involved theory or discourse on the matter, as well as those that did not attempt to measure procedural justice in the context of policing.[6]

Using these criteria, the search for research commenced on February 9, 2017, and was completed on February 23, 2017, resulting in 6,041 manuscripts being identified. Furthermore, due to the temporal gap between the search and the coding process, a recent meta-analysis, comprised of 64 studies (Walters & Bolger, 2019), was used to capture quantitative studies measuring procedural justice between 2017 and 2018–19. Studies that fell within the search criteria were added to the list of manuscripts collected during the initial search. Overall, 6,060 manuscripts were identified as part of the initial search process.

As seen in Figure 7, these 6,060 manuscripts were reduced by removing duplicate[7] and non-English manuscripts, those not related to policing and procedural justice,[8] and those not meeting the inclusion criteria. This process resulted in a total of 176 manuscripts (for a full list, see the Supplemental Materials) that were to be coded for information covering three broad domains: (1) study information,[9] (2) the use of procedural justice,[10] and (3) measurement of procedural justice.[11]

---

[3] This search used Criminal Justice Abstracts, PsychINFO, and Academic Search Complete, accessed through the University of Cincinnati library.

[4] Keywords used: "Procedural Justice" AND "police"; "Procedural Justice" AND "policing"; "Procedural Justice" AND "law enforcement"; "Procedural Justice" AND "measurement"; "Procedural Justice " AND "scale"; "Procedural Justice" AND "fairness"; "Procedural Justice" AND "procedural fairness"; "Procedural Justice" AND "due process"; "Procedural Justice" AND "fundamental justice"; "Procedural Justice" AND "natural justice"; "Procedural Justice" AND "transparency"; "Procedural Justice" AND "Process"; "Procedural Justice" AND "Outcome".

[5] The timeframe for this search was nonrestrictive.

[6] Inclusion of research was not restricted by geography but was restricted to research published/available in English. The endogeneity/exogeneity of procedural justice in this research was not restrictive. Studies were limited to those that examined procedural justice of police or law enforcement officers from the perspective of community members, excluding police perceptions of their own or their peers' procedural justice.

[7] Identified using Google Sheet's "Remove Duplicates" add-on tool, searching APA formatted citations for those sharing the same publication year, authors, and title. A manual search removed additional duplicates.

[8] Manuscript abstracts were reviewed for references to policing or procedural justice – any abstracts or titles producing ambiguity were retained for further investigation for relevance. Then, the entirety of the manuscript was reviewed to ensure it met the inclusion criteria for the study.

[9] Reference information, theoretical backing, geographic location/site, sample size, methodology, dependent variable, independent variables, statistical techniques, hypotheses, broad findings

[10] Whether the study contained a measure of procedural justice, the definition (if any) provided for procedural justice, whether procedural justice was an independent, dependent, or intervening variable.

[11] Whether the measure used was based on a previous measure, the scale construction used, number of items used, the number of items used that were listed items, the reliability of items, the scale

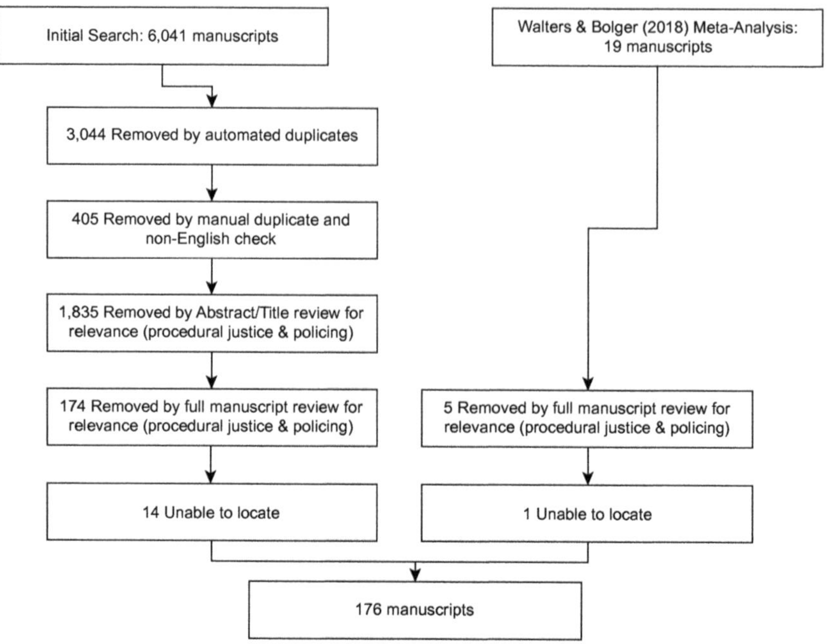

Figure 7 Literature review search narrowing.

The process of coding these 176 manuscripts provided evidence for the diverse use of procedural justice in policing research. The results included the identification of more than 252 unique authors, publications in 67 unique publication outlets (e.g., journals), and the use of an array of sample sizes (ranging from n = 40 to n = 115,260), geographies (e.g., United States, Europe, Australia, Israel, Ghana, Canada), methodologies (e.g., survey/questionnaire/interview, secondary data, observational data gathering), analytic techniques (e.g., linear regression, structural equation modeling, logistic regression), and samples (e.g., community/household respondents, students/youth/juveniles, victims). Furthermore, procedural justice, as a construct, was predominantly used as an independent variable (n = 140), with a variety of scale construction methods (e.g., summative, averaged, indexes),[12] and a wide range of Cronbach's α values (ranging from 0.60 to 0.98).[13]

Additionally, the coding process extracted 1,094 items used to measure procedural justice in these 176 manuscripts.[14] This list was reduced to 769 unique

characteristics, the specified applicability of specific items to Tyler's (2000) four key components – voice, trustworthiness, neutrality, and dignity/respect.

12 The vast majority (n = 114) did not provide details as to how they constructed their scale.

13 A large proportion (n = 69) did not provide details for their scale's reliability.

14 Thirty-two items captured voice (Tyler 2000), 52 trustworthiness, 57 neutrality, and 37 dignity/respect. The remaining items were not articulated as measuring these underlying concepts or measured a related concept, such as quality of decision-making (Tyler & Blader, 2000).

items after exact duplicate items were removed and reduced to 501 when approximate duplicates were removed.[15] This list was further narrowed to 329 items using Dillman and colleagues' (2014) guidelines about item construction.[16] Finally, as a means of reducing the pool but retaining content validity, these 329 items were coded based on their capacity to capture Tyler and Blader's (2000) "quality of decision-making" and "quality of treatment" as well as the item's coding structure (i.e., reverse coded).[17] Within the groups of "quality of decision-making" and "quality of treatment," items that covered very similar content (n = 196) and did not achieve face validity (n = 5) were removed, leading to a final pool of 124 items. These 124 items would be fielded in a random order, using a four-point response scale from "Strongly agree" to "Strongly disagree."[18]

Moving on to Step 3 in the measurement development process, these 124 items were initially piloted, alongside related constructs (e.g., police legitimacy, satisfaction with police, police effectiveness, cooperation with police), on February 6–7, 2019, using Amazon's Mechanical (MTurk) workers, who engage in a variety of tasks – in this case, completion of an online survey – in exchange for nominal payments (see Table 6 for more). Although this type of sampling is considered an online opt-in sample, findings from studies relying on MTurk samples are known to directionally align with results from studies that draw on probability-based methods, especially when such effects are statistically significant (Graham et al., 2021; Thompson & Pickett, 2020). Additionally, such online survey methodologies provide reduced measurement error, satisficing, and social desirability effects compared to traditional paper or phone surveys (Chang & Krosnick, 2009). Furthermore, for the sake of scale development using IRT, the exact representativeness of the sample is not necessarily needed because the items' parameters are not sample-specific; a large and diverse sample is sufficient (Hambleton et al., 1991). Nonetheless, respondents were limited to those living in the United States, were aged 18 years or older, had completed more than 500 "human intelligence tasks" (HITs), and had a successful completion rate of 95 percent or higher (Peer et al.,

[15] Because word choice can influence responses, specific articles (e.g., the, a, an) and noun choices (e.g., police officer, officer) prevented items from being deemed exact duplicate items (AERA et al., 2014).

[16] Dillman and colleagues' (2014) guidelines: items are applicable to all respondents (#4.2), asked one question at a time (#4.2), were technically accurate (#4.3), used simple or familiar words (#4.4), and used as few words as possible to ask the question (#4.7).

[17] Coding the direction of the items was used to help retain negatively worded items in the pool.

[18] The presence of a midpoint (i.e., "neither agree nor disagree") can to lead to an over-selection of such options (Alreck & Settle, 1985; Weems & Onwuegbuzie, 2001), resulting in "false negatives" (Gilljam & Granberg, 1993) an underestimation of attitudes (Warland & Sample, 1973) and reduced internal reliability (Masters, 1974). Therefore, a four-point Likert-type response option was used.

Table 7 Data collection descriptions

	Survey			
	MTurk 1	**MTurk 2**	**MTurk 3**	**YouGov**
Field dates	Feb. 6–7 2019	March 9–10, 2019	April 13–14, 2019	March 2020
Approx. time length	15–18 mins	25–27 mins	20–30 mins	15–20 mins
Incentive	$2.70	$3.75	$3.60	–
N before attention check removal	557	613	627	–
N after attention check removal	493	504	496	1,000
Analytic N (listwise deletion)	493	504	496	971

2014).[19] Because the aim of this construct was to measure perceptions of procedural justice in a general population (not necessarily those who had contact with law enforcement), this sample was sufficient.

Per Step 4, responses to this survey were analyzed using CTT and IRT methodologies. Of the original 557 respondents, 64 were removed for failing one of two attention check items, and one was removed due to missingness on a procedural justice item, leaving an analytic sample of 492 respondents. See Table 8 for a description of this sample's sociodemographic characteristics and comparisons to US Census estimates. Analyses of these items' properties, as well as items from subsequent surveys, will be discussed ahead.

Accordingly, Step 5 was conducted using a second MTurk sample (n = 613, reduced to n = 504 based on attention checks), which was fielded March 9–10, 2019. Using the same methodology, a reduced set of 41 procedural justice items was fielded alongside relevant constructs (see Table 7 for details). A description of the sample is available in Table 8.

As a means of attempting to further reduce these items, a third MTurk sample was surveyed (n = 627, reduced to n = 496 based on attention checks) on April

[19] A HIT is "a question that needs an answer. A HIT represents a single, self-contained, virtual task that a Worker can work on, submit an answer, and collect a reward for completing. HITs are created by Requester customers in order to be completed by Worker customers" (Amazon Mechanical Turk, 2018).

Table 8 Descriptive statistics

	MTurk 1 (n = 493)	MTurk 2 (n = 504)	MTurk 3 (n = 496)	YouGov[#] (n = 971)		US Population Estimate[+]
	Mean (SD)/%	Mean (SD)/%	Mean (SD)/%	Mean (SD)/%	Range	%
Age	36.47 (9.55)	38.25 (11.27)	36.49 (11.25)	48.89 (18.15)	19–73	
Female (%)	37.7	41.7	46.6	51.3	0–1	50.80
Race						
White (%)	75.5	78.8	70.2	68.52	0–1	76.60
Black (%)	14.2	6.7	9.5	12.03	0–1	13.40
Other (%)	10.3	14.5	20.3	7.09	0–1	–
Hispanic/Latino (%)	15.2	3.0	4.6	12.36	0–1	18.10
Education	4.27 (1.31)	4.26 (1.29)	4.42 (1.24)	3.33 (1.51)	1–7	–
Income	4.07 (1.44)	4.14 (1.54)	4.20 (1.58)	5.74 (3.55)	1–7	–
Full-time employment (%)	74.4	72.0	72.4	33.8	0–1	63[^]
Married (%)	40.6	41.5	40.5	43.9	0–1	39.50
Republican (%)	26.6	23.4	28.8	26.2	0–1	25[**]
Police effectiveness	3.90 (0.95)	3.90 (0.89)	3.91 (0.84)	3.66 (1.05)	1–5	–
Satisfaction with police	3.80 (0.91)	3.77 (0.86)	3.75 (0.82)	3.68 (0.93)	1–5	–

Table 8 (cont.)

	MTurk 1 (n = 493)	MTurk 2 (n = 504)	MTurk 3 (n = 496)	YouGov (n = 971)		US Population Estimate
	Mean (SD)/%	**Mean (SD)/%**	**Mean (SD)/%**	**Mean (SD)/%**	**Range**	**%**
Cooperation with police	3.21 (0.58)	3.30 (0.59)	3.29 (0.53)	3.34 (0.67)	1–4	–
Police legitimacy	2.69 (1.05)	2.53 (1.03)	3.46 (0.98)	3.50 (0.96)	1–5	–
Law legitimacy	2.75 (0.69)	2.69 (0.83)	3.36 (0.77)	3.45 (0.75)	1–5	–

* Percentages may not sum to 100 percent due to rounding.

** (Gallup, 2019 – as of January 22–February 10, 2019).

^ In civilian labor force, 16+.

+ The US Census estimates July 1, 2018.

weighted data.

13–14, 2019. A reduced set of 29 procedural justice items was fielded using the same methodologies just described (see Table 7 for details). The sample is described in more detail in Table 8.

Finally, as a means of validating the results from the third MTurk sample, a matched opt-in online national sample of respondents (n = 1,000) was commissioned through YouGov in March 2020. Derived from their pool of more than 6 million international panelists across 38 countries, YouGov uses a multistage propensity score matching and weighting process to produce samples that approximate those of large probability-based samples (see Rivers, 2007 for more). YouGov's sample-matching approach has been found to produce high-quality samples (Ansolabehere & Schaffner, 2014; Simmons & Bobo, 2015) as well as estimates in the same direction and similar magnitude as large probability-based samples (Graham et al., 2021). In this sample of respondents, YouGov matched US panelists to the 2017 American Community Survey based on gender, age, race, and education. These cases were then weighted using propensity scores based on age, gender, race/ethnicity, education, and region. Finally, the weights were post-stratified based on 2016 presidential vote choice, age, race, and education to produce the final weights. All analyses with the YouGov data use these provided weights. See Tables 7 and 8 for details on this sample.

4.3 Analytic Strategy

Each sample's procedural justice items underwent similar analytic processes. The procedure started by examining the samples' procedural justice items' internal reliability (i.e., Cronbach's α) as a scale and subjecting all procedural justice items to EFA, using principal component analysis and promax rotation. Next, items were assessed using IRT analytic methods (for more on IRT methods, see de Ayala, 2009). As mentioned, this item-level analysis is essential for scale development (beyond CTT methods) because it provides for the nonlinear modeling of a latent construct/trait (θ) based on items (i) that may vary in difficulty (b_i) and capacity to discriminate (a_i) between respondents of differing levels of a characteristic on the underlying construct or trait, such as ability (de Ayala, 2009; Hambleton & Jones, 1993; Hambleton et al., 1991). This type of modeling typically assumes (1) unidimensionality (although there are multidimensional models), (2) local independence of items and respondent ability, (3) item invariance, and (4) monotonicity of the trait (θ) (de Ayala, 2009; Hambleton et al., 1991).

Although there are multiple modeling strategies under the IRT framework (e.g., Rasch, one-parameter logistic, two-parameter logistic), for this Element, the graded response model (GRM) (Samejima, 1969) is most appropriate given the polytomous and ordered response options of these items ($x_i = 0, 1, \ldots, m_i$) that are accommodated within this model. This model estimates the probability that a respondent selects a specific response category for an item while also allowing for items within the scale to vary in their capacity to discriminate between individuals (a_i) and in their difficulty (b_i). Specifically, the one-dimensional homogenous GRM (Samejima, 1969; see also Hambleton et al., 1991) calculates the probability of selecting a specific response option ($P_{x_i}(\theta)$), using the following:

$$P_{x_i}(\theta) = P^*_{x_i}(\theta) - P^*_{x_i+1}(\theta), \quad \text{in which } P^*_{x_i}(\theta) = \frac{e^{Da_i(\theta - b_{x_i})}}{1 + e^{Da_i(\theta - b_{x_i})}},$$

where a_i is the discrimination parameter, b_{x_i} is the difficulty for category m_i, and D is a scaling factor (usually equal to 1.7) to approximate a normal ogive function.[20]

In short, preferred scales, from the perspective of IRT, are those with items that have higher discrimination parameters (a_i) and those with a broad range of difficulty (b_i) over the span of θ (Yang & Kao, 2014). Additionally, when evaluating items to comprise a scale, items are only useful for retention if they (1) provide the capacity for precise estimates along the underlying dimension (θ) – that is, they have more "information" – and (2) these items do not demonstrate differential item functioning (DIF) between groups – that is, items should be invariant (assumption #3; Hambleton et al., 1991; Osterlind & Everson, 2009). Stated in other terms, people from different groups (e.g., race, gender) but with the same ability (or level of an underlying trait) should have the same probability of getting an item right. As such, the discrimination, difficulty, information, and DIF of items were assessed.[21]

---

20 The R' ltm package models this function using the command grm as: *logit(γ_ik) = beta_i z – beta_ik*, where *γ_{ik}* denotes the cumulative probability of a response in category *k*th or lower to the *i*th item, given the latent ability *z*. If constrained = TRUE it is assumed that *β_i = β* for all *i*. If IRT. param = TRUE, then the parameters estimates are reported under the usual IRT parameterization – that is, *logit (γ_ik) = beta_i (z – beta_ik^*)*, where *beta_ik^* = beta_ik / beta_i*. The fit of the model is based on approximate marginal maximum likelihood, using the Gauss–Hermite quadrature rule for the approximation of the required integrals.

21 Differential item functioning was assessed using a significance-based two-stage likelihood ratio test approach with "anchor items" (see Meade & Wright, 2012), which compares nested models (i.e., baseline/constrained versus comparison). The first model is a constrained model, treating "all others as anchors" (i.e., all item parameters are estimated equivalently across groups). The second model treats the top five non-DIF items as anchors (i.e., equal across groups) to estimate DIF. Significant differences in the likelihood value of items, using a chi-squared distribution, indicate DIF (Meade & Wright, 2012). Limiting DIF improves the ability of meaningfully assessing group differences (i.e., potential test bias) at the scale level (Osterlind & Everson, 2009).

Still, further checks on the final scale's validity and reliability are necessary to assess the scale's utility. As such, the finalized scale underwent several analyses. To assess the scale's internal reliability – that all items within the scale measure the same construct – Cronbach's α is computed (Singleton & Straits, 2010). Next, we assess the scale's face validity – that it appears to measure the construct it alleges – and its content validity – that it captures the meaning of the construct in its entirety – through comparisons of the scale to its definition and the theoretical dimensions of procedural justice as described by Tyler and Blader (2000) (Singleton & Straits, 2010). The scale's content validity is assessed by examining its convergent validity – that it correlates with theoretically related measures – using satisfaction with police, cooperation with police, and police effectiveness, as well as its discriminant validity – that it does not correlate with theoretically unrelated measures – using age, income, education, belief in a dangerous world, anger about crime, 2016 vote choice, and punitive attitudes about the criminal justice system (for more on validity, see Singleton & Straits, 2010). Furthermore, to assess the predictive validity of our scale – that it is associated with values of theoretically subsequent constructs – we examine its relationship to perceived police legitimacy, satisfaction with police, cooperation with police, and effectiveness of police with structural equation modeling (Messick, 1995). All items used in these scales and their response options are provided in the Supplemental Materials.

4.4 Results: Creating the Graham et al. 10-Item Scale

Given that our measure of procedural justice was evaluated using a series of iterative surveys, the results that follow unfold similarly. We start with the CTT and IRT analyses of the 124 items in the first survey. Next, we describe the CTT and IRT results of the 41 items retained and fielded within the second survey. Subsequently, we turn to the CTT and IRT results of the 29 retained items fielded in the third survey. We then propose a 10-item scale to measure procedural justice in policing, presenting CTT and IRT evidence to suggest its validity and reliability. Finally, we present the CTT and IRT results (with additional validity and reliability analyses) of our 10-item scale, which was fielded using a national-level opt-in YouGov survey to validate our scale.

Again, this 10-item scale of procedural justice in policing has been constructed using systematic modern psychometric methods. Accordingly, we propose that it should be the preferred measure of procedural justice in policing in all subsequent research collecting primary data. Such a measure merits an identifiable name. In this regard, we mirror the label given to "Grasmick et al. Self-Control Scale."

Thus we term our 10-item measure as the "Graham et al. Procedural Justice in Policing Scale," or, for brevity, we recommend the "Graham et al. Scale."

4.4.1 Pilot Survey and Removing Items from the Pool

Following the fielding of the first survey, the internal reliability of the 124 items was estimated, resulting in a Cronbach's α of 0.992. Despite this high alpha, a scale of 124 items is of minimal utility because of its exorbitant length and heavy respondent burden. To move forward, an EFA was estimated for these 124 items, resulting in eight factors with an eigenvalue greater than 1, explaining 52.59 percent of the total variance within the first factor.[22] Notably, all 27 reverse-coded items loaded onto their own distinct factor. This finding suggests that procedural justice and procedural injustice may be two distinct underlying constructs, not just poles on the same continuum. Conversely, this may also reflect methods variance. We return to this issue in Section 6.

Next, these 124 items were analyzed using the IRT methodologies described earlier in this Element. In addition to the GRM, analyses also examined the potential fit related to the partial credit model (PCM) (Masters, 1982), a two-dimensional graded response model without factor covariance (2D-GRM w/o Cov), and a two-dimensional graded response model with factor covariance (2D-GRM w/ Cov) (de Ayala, 1994). Model fit (AIC) (Akaike, 1974) suggested that the 2D-GRM w/ Cov was the best-fitting model that aligns with the multiple dimensions identified in the EFA.[23] Still, analyses from all three GRMs provided insight into the discrimination and difficulty of these items. Over three iterations, items with low discrimination were removed from the pool of potential items, and models were reestimated. This iterative process was used to ensure that items were not inadvertently removed due to other poorly performing items within the pool.

The remaining items were examined for DIF across sex, education, income, employment, political identity, marital status, if the respondent had been stopped by the police in the previous year, if the respondent had called the police for help in the previous year, age, and race.[24] Hambleton and colleagues

---

[22] The EFA factors rotated using oblique (promax) rotation to account for potentially correlated factors, evidenced in the −.531 correlation between the first and second factors (Osborne, 2015). Factor retention was based on the Kaiser (1960) threshold – an eigenvalue of 1 or greater.

[23] GRM AIC = 100,174.0; PCM AIC = 109,240.7; 2D-GRM w/o Cov AIC = 93,544.2; 2D-GRM w/ Cov AIC = 93,367.9.

[24] Because two dimensions were presumed at this point, DIF was examined independently for each factor.

(1991) caution that although invariance is not an "all-or-none property in the population and can never be observed in the strict sense," tests of invariance or DIF are assessing the "'degree' to which it holds when we use samples of test data," which is a bit more "subjective" (p. 24). To be conservative, items that exhibited DIF across three or fewer of these characteristics were retained (n = 41). Notably, all 27 reverse-coded items exhibited DIF across four or more of the examined characteristics and were dropped from the pool.

Moving to the second survey, 41 items were retained to measure procedural justice. After fielding this survey, similar analyses were performed. The Cronbach's α for the 41 items was 0.986, and an EFA identified two factors with eigenvalues greater than 1 – the first reflecting the construct of procedural justice and the second exhibiting a construct similar to Tyler's (2000) idea of "voice."[25] As with the first set of items, multiple IRT modeling strategies were estimated in search of the best-fitting model, including multidimensional GRMs, given the results of the EFA. Based on the AIC, the best-fitting model was the 2D-GRM w/ Cov.[26] Additionally, item discriminations were examined across all three GRMs. Across all three models, all items demonstrated relatively high discrimination, so no items were removed from the pool based on this analysis. Next, these items were examined for DIF using the aforementioned characteristics, with items exhibiting DIF with four or fewer characteristics retained (n = 29).

The third survey was fielded with the remaining 29 items, and similar analyses were undertaken. The Cronbach's α for these items was 0.973, with the EFA producing two factors with eigenvalues greater than 1.[27] The first factor reflected the construct of procedural justice, while the second factor was unclear as to its underlying construct. Another EFA was estimated, forcing all items onto one factor, which produced factor loadings ranging between 0.678 and 0.803, which are acceptable (Nunnally & Bernstein, 1978). All 29 items were retained and underwent IRT analyses. Only the PCM and the one-dimensional GRM were estimated, given the findings of the EFA. Here, the best-fitting model, based on AIC, was the one-dimensional GRM.[28] When examining the items' discrimination parameters, none exhibited low discrimination relative to the other items remaining in the pool. As such, all items were examined for DIF,

[25] Although two factors were suggested (having eigenvalues over 1; Kaiser, 1960), the second factor's eigenvalue was 1.062, barely beyond the threshold of 1. Cliff (1988) and others (e.g., Zwick & Velicer, 1986) note such cutoffs can overestimate the number of present factors.

[26] GRM AIC = 28,841.8; PCM AIC = 30,490.4; 2D-GRM w/o Cov AIC = 29,413.7; 2D-GRM w/ Cov IC = 28,657.7.

[27] The second factor's eigenvalue was 1.094, barely above the Kaiser (1960) threshold.

[28] GRM AIC = 22,076.8; PCM AIC = 22,866.5.

with several exhibiting DIF. Still, as Hambleton and colleagues (1991) note, such invariance can be subjective; future research can continue to examine this matter in the case of procedural justice. Nonetheless, all items were retained for the sake of further validation.

4.4.2 Proposing a 10-Item Scale

Our proposed 10-item scale measuring procedural justice was drawn from these 29 items. The selection of items was guided theoretically by Tyler and Blader's (2000) two-component model, Tyler's four key elements, and our construct's definition. Equally important, the scale was developed using the items' statistical capacity for discrimination, range of threshold difficulty, and invariance as guiding elements. These statistical analyses were based on three Amazon MTurk surveys. As reported in Section 4.4.3, a final check on the scale's reliability and validity was conducted using a national-level YouGov survey. The 10-item Graham et al. scale is presented in Table 9. Each item follows the stem "The police in my community … ".

To bolster content validity, all 29 items were first sorted into whether they represented Tyler and Blader's (2000) "quality of treatment" or "quality of decision-making." Recall that the quality of treatment focuses on the interpersonal experience, whereas the quality of decision-making focuses on "the manner in which decisions are made" (Tyler & Blader, 2000, p. 103). We selected the top five items from each of these two groups (analyzed across all 29 items used in each of the three MTurk surveys; see Table 9 for categorization), ensuring that Tyler's (2000) four key elements – voice, neutrality, trustworthiness, and dignity/respect – were also represented within these items. Table 9 identifies which group items fall into (quality of treatment; quality of decision-making). These items had, in combination, the highest discrimination (all exhibited "very high" discrimination = > 1.7; Baker, 2001), the broadest range of difficulty (spaced between −3 and +3; Baker, 2001), and the least invariance. Our proposed 10 items are presented in Table 9.

Given our proposed 10-item scale, retrospective reliability and validity analyses of these 10 items were examined using data from all three fielded MTurk surveys. As seen in Table 10, regardless of the survey, the scale had high internal reliability (i.e., Cronbach's α) and a broad range of item difficulty. Likewise, regardless of the survey, these items exhibited good factor loadings (see Table 11) and high relative item discriminations (see Table 12). Notably, these GRMs demonstrate consistent and robust model fit as seen in the low root mean square error of approximation (RMSEA) values (below the standard cutoff of 0.05; Browne & Cudeck, 1993; Steiger, 1990), high comparative fit index (CFI) (Bentler, 1990) and Tucker–Lewis index (TLI) (Tucker & Lewis,

Table 9 Graham et al.'s 10-item procedural justice in policing scale

Stem: "The police in my community … "				
Quality of treatment	Trustwortdiness	Dignity/Respect	Voice	Neutrality
1. Are usually courteous.	X			
2. Are usually honest.	X			
3. Would treat you with respect if you had contact with them for any reason.		X		
4. Respect your basic rights.		X		
5. Usually treat people with respect.		X		
Quality of decision-making				
6. Take people's needs into consideration.			X	
7. Give people opportunities to explain their situation.			X	
8. Try to be fair.				X
9. Make decisions about what to do in fair ways.				X
10. Can be trusted.				X

Table 10 Scale reliabilities and item threshold difficulty ranges

Scale reliabilities (Cronbach's α)			
MTurk 1	MTurk 2	MTurk 3	YouGov
0.952	0.950	0.934	0.958
Item threshold difficulty ranges			
−2.468 to 0.877	−2.156 to 1.111	−2.445 to 0.908	−1.876 to 0.882

Table 11 Scale factor loadings by survey*: Graham et al.'s 10-item procedural justice scale

Items	**MTurk 1 N = 493**	**MTurk 2 N = 504**	**MTurk 3 N = 496**	**YouGov N = 971**
"The police in my community …"				
1. Are usually courteous.	0.829	0.786	0.743	0.821
2. Are usually honest.	0.828	0.837	0.802	0.847
3. Would treat you with respect if you had contact with them for any reason.	0.734	0.806	0.773	0.822
4. Respect your basic rights.	0.812	0.825	0.741	0.853
5. Usually treat people with respect.	0.815	0.880	0.777	0.831
6. Take people's needs into consideration.	0.822	0.801	0.737	0.806
7. Give people opportunities to explain their situation.	0.801	0.750	0.731	0.830
8. Make decisions about what to do in fair ways.	0.818	0.781	0.771	0.849
9. Try to be fair.	0.864	0.833	0.788	0.854
10. Can be trusted.	0.840	0.809	0.797	0.834
Factor 1 Eigenvalue	6.673	6.588	5.872	6.974
% of Explained Variance	66.726	65.877	58.717	69.739

* Only loadings greater than 0.4 are presented.

1973) values (above the standard cutoffs of 0.95; Bentler & Bonett, 1980; Hu & Bentler, 1999), and low standardized root mean square residual (SRMSR) (below the standard cutoff of 0.05; Maydeu-Olivares, 2013).

Table 12 One-dimensional graded response model discrimination by survey – Graham et al. 10-Item Procedural Justice Scale

Items	**MTurk 1** **N = 493**	**MTurk 2** **N = 504**	**MTurk 3** **N = 496**	**YouGov** **N = 971**
"The police in my community … "				
1. Are usually courteous.	3.598	2.790	2.503	3.638
2. Are usually honest.	3.450	3.563	3.059	4.056
3. Would treat you with respect if you had contact with them for any reason.	2.465	3.090	2.756	3.761
4. Respect your basic rights.	3.272	3.462	2.505	4.092
5. Usually treat people with respect.	3.281	4.838	2.864	3.779
6. Take people's needs into consideration.	3.414	3.028	2.380	3.377
7. Give people opportunities to explain their situation.	3.003	2.511	2.305	3.722
8. Try to be fair.	4.315	3.616	2.989	4.239
9. Make decisions about what to do in fair ways.	3.281	2.820	2.680	4.248
10. Can be trusted.	3.629	3.016	2.997	3.860
RMSEA (CI)	0.020 (0–0.049)	0.040 (0.013–0.064)	0.063 (0.042–0.084)	0.040 (0.024–0.056)
CFI/TLI	0.997/0.995	0.988/0.980	0.964/0.939	0.990/0.984
SRMSR	0.023	0.023	0.031	0.022

To provide additional evidence regarding the validity of the proposed scale, it was subjected to correlational analyses with items related to procedural justice (i.e., convergent validity) and items not related to procedural justice (i.e., discriminant validity). The production of convergent validity is demonstrated with strong correlations to related measures, whereas discriminant validity is ascertained through weak correlations to unrelated measures (Singleton & Straits, 2010). As seen in Table 13, the proposed scale performed as expected. Across the MTurk-based scales, correlations with satisfaction with police ranged from $r = 0.732$ to $r = 0.779$, with police effectiveness ranging from $r = 0.757$ to $r = 0.831$, and with cooperation with police ranging from $r = 0.474$ to $r = 0.586$.[29] This pattern of high correlations provides evidence of the scale possessing convergent validity.

In contrast, across the MTurk-based measures of variables unrelated to policing outcomes, the correlations were low. These consistent findings are evidence of discriminant validity. Thus the scale's correlations with age ranged from $r = -0.024$ to $r = 0.141$, with education ranging from $r = -0.020$ to $r = 0.065$, with income ranging from $r = 0.026$ to 0.191, with libertarianism ranging from $r = 0.021$ to $r = 0.139$, with racial resentment ranging from $r = 0.150$ to $r = 0.192$, with punitiveness in the criminal justice system ranging from $r = 0.143$ to $r = 0.151$, with belief in a dangerous world $r = 0.035$, with anger about crime $r = 0.126$, with racial sympathy $r = -0.086$, with 2020 likely vote choice $r = 0.282$, and with Black Lives Matter support $r = -0.191$.

4.4.3 Finalizing Our 10-Item Graham et al. Scale

Given the robust findings of our proposed 10-item scale, and as recommended by psychology (AERA et al., 2014), we sought to validate our scale by completing another test with just our final items. This final form of validation was conducted using a nationwide matched opt-in online sample commissioned through YouGov.

Following the fielding of these 10 items in the YouGov survey, similar CTT and IRT analyses were undertaken. These analyses produced a scale of high internal reliability ($\alpha = 0.958$; see Table 10), broad difficulty (difficulty [b_i] between −1.876 and 0.882; see Table 10), good factor loadings (loadings between 0.806 and 0.854; see Table 11), high discrimination parameters

[29] Arguably, police effectiveness (instrumental judgment) and procedural justice (normative judgment) are competing constructs as antecedents of legitimacy. Still, we anticipate them being highly correlated as both significantly influence legitimacy (e.g., Sunshine & Tyler, 2003a). As we demonstrate later, these constructs are distinct in our data despite their high correlations.

Table 13 Correlation matrix – Graham et al. 10-Item Procedural Justice Scale

	MTurk 1	MTurk 2	MTurk 3	YouGov
Age	−0.024	0.029	0.141**	0.173***
Education	0.065	0.054	−0.020	0.078*
Income	0.077	0.191***	0.026	0.121***
Libertarianism	0.021	0.139**	–	–
Racial resentment	0.167***	0.150***	0.192***	–
Racial sympathy	–	–	−0.086	–
Black Lives Matter support	−0.191***	–	–	–
2016 Trump voter	–	–	–	0.283***
Likely 2020 Trump voter	0.282***	–	–	–
Dangerous world beliefs	–	0.035	–	0.001
Anger about crime	–	0.126**	–	0.020
CJS punitiveness	–	0.143**	0.151***	0.162***
Police effectiveness	0.831***	0.826***	0.757***	0.483***
Satisfaction with police	0.779***	0.764***	0.732***	0.676***
Cooperation with police	0.624***	0.586***	0.474***	0.446***
Police legitimacy	0.376***	0.540***	0.386***	0.404***
Law legitimacy	0.116**	0.460***	0.254***	0.421***

*$p < 0.05$; **$p < 0.01$; ***$p < 0.001$

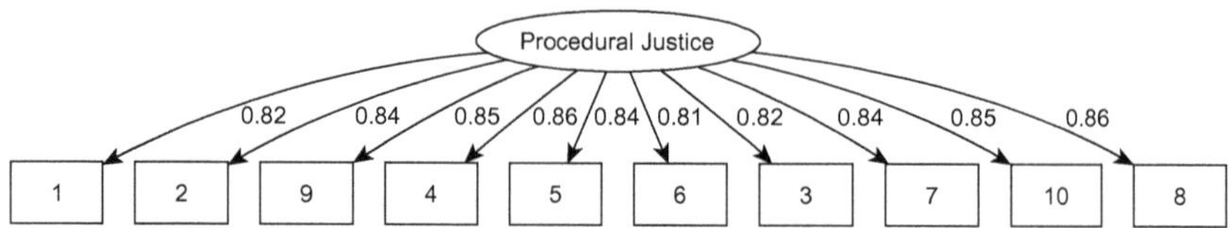

Figure 8 CFA of Graham et al. scale – YouGov sample (N = 761).
Note: All values are standardized values.

(discrimination [a_i] between 3.377 and 4.248; see Table 12), and adequate test information (< 10) across the span of θ.[30] These analyses thus point to evidence suggesting strong reliability and construct validity. As an additional check on the scale's construct validity, the items were subjected to a CFA, with all items used to measure the latent construct of procedural justice. As seen in Figure 8, all items performed as anticipated, with indications of adequate model fit (CFI = 0.977; TLI = 0.971; RMSEA = 0.078 (90% CI = 0.067 to 0.088); SRMR = 0.021).

The scale was also subjected to group invariance testing using gender, race (white/all others), and educational attainment (split between a two-year degree or less and a four-year degree or more) to examine whether the scale operated differentially for subgroups. That is, we assessed whether the scale had the same effects across respondent characteristics – whether it "worked" the same way regardless of whether a person was male or female, white or non-white, or more educated or less. Separate and apart from examining DIF, this invariance analysis is important for two key reasons. First, analytically, if the scale operates with non-invariance, subsequent analysis should account for this by freely estimating certain item loadings, intercepts, or residuals. Second, and more substantively, if a scale operates non-invariantly between groups, it suggests a different understanding or interpretation of a construct between groups, which has implications for the measurement and understanding of the construct.

To test for invariance (e.g., between males vs. females), we first model the construct in a CFA freely estimating factor loadings, intercepts, and residuals for both groups (i.e., configural model), which will serve as a comparison for subsequent restricted models (Putnick & Bornstein, 2016). Next, we estimate a CFA model that constrains factor loadings to be equivalent between groups (i.e.,

[30] As a further check on this scale's psychometric properties, it was subjected to nonparametric IRT analysis (Mokken (1971) model of monotone homogeneity), finding strong scalability coefficients (> 0.5) across all items, and three items with significant, minor violations of latent monotonicity ("usually treat people with respect"; "take people's needs into consideration"; "try to be fair").

metric model). This metric model is compared to the configural model to understand if the metric model is statistically similar to the configural model. If it is, the construct is said to have metric invariance (Putnick & Bornstein, 2016).

If these models are statistically dissimilar, modification indices can be examined to identify potential factor loadings that should be estimated freely between groups in order to achieve similar models (Putnick & Bornstein, 2016). Once the metric model is adjusted to be statistically similar, it can be said to have achieved partial metric invariance (Putnick & Bornstein, 2016). From here, we estimate a third CFA model, which fixes factor loadings and intercepts to be equal between groups (i.e., scalar model). This scalar model is compared to the less restrictive (and, if needed, modified) configural model for statistical similarity (Putnick & Bornstein, 2016). If statistically similar, the construct is said to have achieved scalar invariance (Putnick & Bornstein, 2016). However, if these two models are dissimilar, modifications should be made until they reach similarity. Once achieving this similarity, the construct can be said to have partial scalar invariance (Putnick & Bornstein, 2016).

This analysis identified partial metric variance with regard to gender, which was able to be rectified by freely estimating the factor loadings for item 6 between groups. Otherwise, once addressing item 6's loadings, the scale exhibited metric and scalar invariance by gender. For race, the scale again had partial metric variance, which was correctable by freely estimating the factor loadings for items 7 and 10. Upon this adjustment, the scale exhibited metric and scalar invariance. Finally, concerning educational attainment, the scale exhibited partial metric invariance, which was correctable by freely estimating factor loadings for items 5, 6, and 10. Upon freeing these factor loadings, the scale exhibited metric and scalar invariance. As such, the scale appears to largely function similarly across these sociodemographic groups.

This final scale exhibited strong face validity and content validity by capturing Tyler and Blader's (2000) "quality of decision-making" and "quality of treatment" (see Table 9 for categorizations), Tyler's (2000) four key elements (voice, neutrality, trustworthiness, and dignity/respect), as well as our definition of procedural justice in policing – the perception of fairness of the procedures and processes used by police or law enforcement officers from the perspective of community members. This scale also exhibited convergent validity with satisfaction with police ($r = 0.676$), cooperation ($r = 0.446$), and effectiveness ($r = 0.483$; see Table 13), as well as discriminant validity from age ($r = 0.173$), income ($r = 0.121$), education ($r = 0.078$), 2016 vote choice ($r = 0.283$), belief in a dangerous world ($r = 0.001$), anger about crime ($r = 0.020$), and punitiveness of the criminal justice system ($r = 0.162$; see Table 13).

As a further check on the discriminant validity of our scale, these items and items used to measure police legitimacy (a subsequent variable within the process-based model; Trinkner et al., 2018) were subjected to EFA within the same EFA. As seen in Table 14, Graham et al. scale items loaded onto their own independent factor, separate from items used to measure police legitimacy. Furthermore, based on a separate EFA, our measure of procedural justice was

Table 14 Exploratory factor analysis of Graham et al.'s 10-item procedural justice policing scale with police legitimacy

Items	**YouGov N = 970**	
Procedural justice		
"The police in my community … "		
1. Are usually courteous.	0.811	
2. Are usually honest.	0.842	
3. Would treat you with respect if you had contact with them for any reason.	0.809	
4. Respect your basic rights.	0.859	
5. Usually treat people with respect.	0.851	
6. Take people's needs into consideration.	0.820	
7. Give people opportunities to explain their situation.	0.828	
8. Try to be fair.	0.875	
9. Make decisions about what to do in fair ways.	0.858	
10. Can be trusted.	0.816	
Police legitimacy[a]		
1. You should support the decision made by police officers even when you disagree with them.		0.693
2. You should do what the police tell you even if you do not understand or agree with the reasons.		0.843
3. The police in your community are legitimate authorities, and you should do what they tell you to do.		0.886

Table 14 (cont.)

Items	YouGov N = 970	
4. You should do what the police tell you to do even if you do not like how they treat you.		0.861
5. The police stand up for values that are important to you.		0.714
6. You generally support how the police act in your community.		0.722
7. The police usually act in ways consistent with your own ideas about what is right and wrong.		0.701
Eigenvalues	7.158	4.252
% of explained variance	42.107	25.012

* Only loadings greater than 0.4 are presented; promax rotation; a – in the Supplemental Materials, Legitimacy was also broken into Trinkner et al.'s (2018) component parts of "Duty to Obey" and "Normative Alignment," with substantively similar findings.

also distinct from police effectiveness (see Supplemental Materials). Additionally, all items in the Graham et al. scale continued to maintain high factor loadings in the presence of these other items, which also points to evidence of discriminant validity.

Finally, the predictive validity of the Graham et al. scale was assessed in two ways. First, it was used in a series of linear (OLS) models to predict police legitimacy, cooperation with police, satisfaction with police – expected outcomes of procedural justice, based on the process-based model – controlling for sociodemographic characteristics of respondents. As seen in Table 15, the Graham et al. procedural justice scale performed as anticipated, with significant associations with all three outcomes.

Second, the Graham et al. scale was used as the most exogenous variable in a structural equation model. As seen in Figure 9, procedural justice was significantly and directly associated with increases in perceptions of police legitimacy – as anticipated by the prior theorizing (RMSEA = 0.079 [90% CI = 0.077 to 0.082]; CFI = 0.883; TLI = 0.874; SRMR = 0.213).[31] Furthermore, police

[31] Allowing for shared variance between several items used to measure cooperation, legitimacy, and effectiveness (within their respective construct) provided for a better-fitting model (RMSEA 0.050 [90% CI = 0.048 to 0.053]; CFI = 0.935; TLI = 0.928; SRMR = 0.183).

Table 15 OLS regression models – YouGov sample

	Legitimacy[a] (N = 763)			Cooperation (N = 763)			Satisfaction (N = 762)		
	b	**SE**	**β**	**b**	**SE**	**β**	**b**	**SE**	**β**
Procedural justice	0.382	0.033	0.385***	0.218	0.024	0.324***	0.540	0.028	0.557***
Contacted police (Y)	0.039	0.075	0.016	−0.048	0.051	−0.030	−0.110	0.058	−0.048
Stopped by police (Y)	−0.120	0.087	−0.044	0.080	0.059	0.043	0.210	0.068	0.079**
Age	0.011	0.002	0.198***	0.008	0.001	0.223***	0.006	0.001	0.112***
Male	−0.065	0.060	−0.034	−0.128	0.041	−0.099**	−.042	0.047	−0.023
White	0.143	0.069	0.068*	−0.014	0.047	−0.010	0.028	0.054	0.014
Education	0.087	0.069	0.042	−0.021	0.047	−0.015	−0.031	0.054	−0.015
Income	−0.005	0.009	−0.019	0.005	0.006	0.027	0.010	0.007	0.037
Conservativism	0.122	0.039	0.108**	0.020	0.027	0.026	0.046	0.031	0.042
Legitimacy[a]	–	–	–	0.090	0.025	0.133***	0.189	0.028	0.193***
Intercept	2.850	0.230	–	2.599	0.171	–	2.423	0.196	–
Adjusted R-squared		0.264			0.267			0.533	

Note: Weighted; $*p < 0.05$; $**p < 0.01$; $***p < 0.001$; a – In the Supplemental Materials, Legitimacy was also broken into Trinkner et al.'s (2018) component parts of "Duty to Obey" and "Normative Alignment," with substantively similar findings.

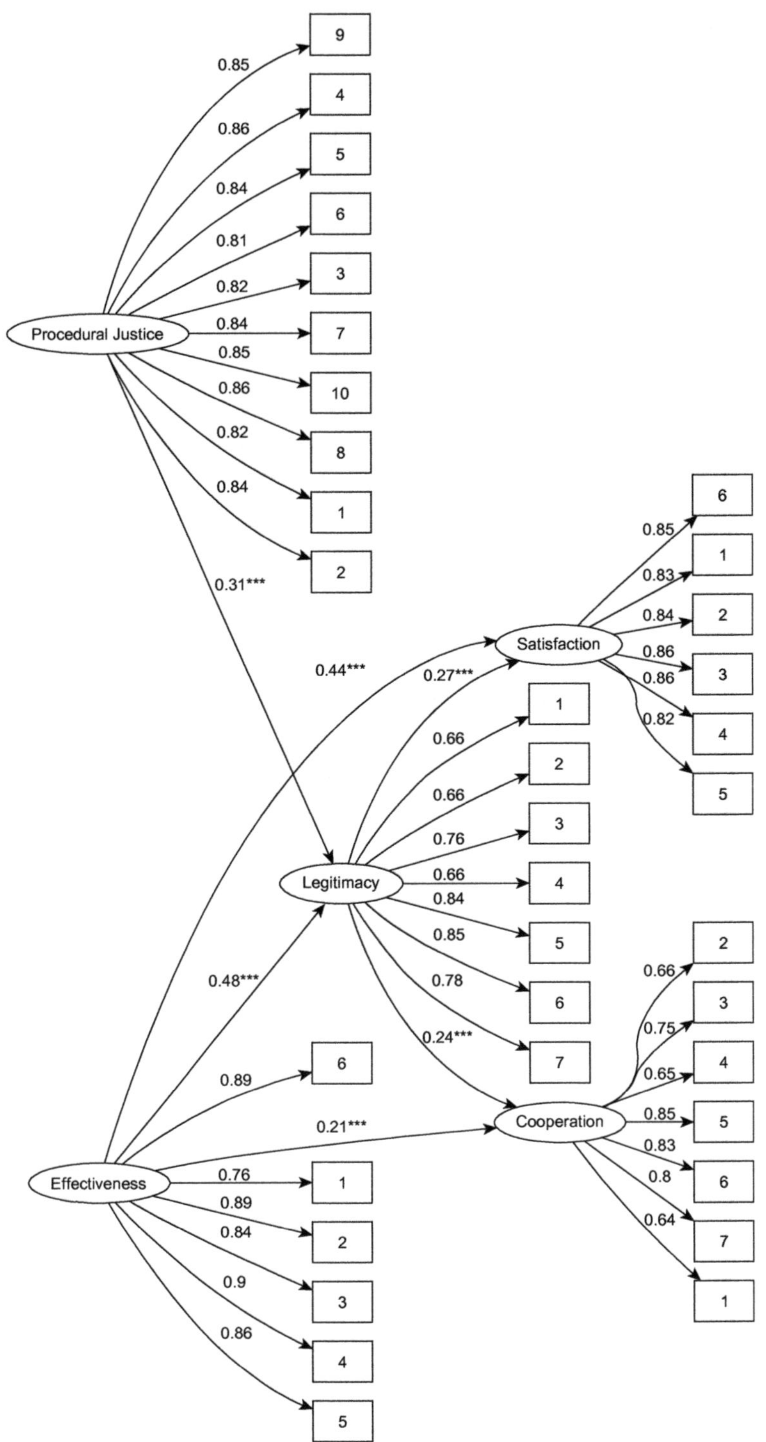

Figure 9 Structural equation model of the process-based model – YouGov Sample (N = 761).

legitimacy and perceived police effectiveness were significantly associated with satisfaction with police as well as cooperation with police, which comports with prior theorization. Therefore, based on these two sets of analyses, there is a strong case for the predictive validity of the Graham et al. scale.

4.5 Conclusion

Starting with 1,094 items derived from 176 studies, Section 4 demonstrated the process of "criminometrics" that was used to reach a 10-item scale of procedural justice in policing using modern psychometric methods. The "Graham et al. Procedural Justice Scale in Policing" has indicators of strong reliability and evidence of validity at both the item and scale levels. To our knowledge, this is the first measure of a criminological construct to be developed using modern psychometric methods from start to finish. More broadly, the process described in this section provides a pioneering effort to provide a template to be employed in criminology's future measurement of theoretical constructs. It opens a new frontier for budding scholars to follow our case study and develop their own scales or measures constructed with modern psychometric methods.

5 Adjudication of Existing Measures

Thus far, we have used modern psychometric methods to arrive at our 10-item scale of procedural justice in policing – the Graham et al. scale. Importantly, several other measures of procedural justice in policing exist – none developed using the complete repertoire of modern psychometric methods. They have been used to study a host of relationships, producing a large body of literature on procedural justice. This reality raises the possibility that the lengthy process used to construct our 10-item scale has simply reinvented the wheel. It is possible that existing measures may, in the end, prove to be just as sufficient as the one we have constructed.

The quality of existing measures, however, cannot be known if no benchmark exists against which to compare them. One value of a systematically and psychometrically derived measure is that it can serve as an evaluative tool. It can reveal the merits of existing scales relative to newly developed scales and relative to one another. In this section, we furnish an example of how such a comparison might be undertaken, comparing two of the most prominent measures with our scale. This endeavor is substantively important in its own right, but it also serves as an example of how other psychometrically developed measures can be employed to assess the status of scales measuring key criminological constructs.

5.1 Comparisons with Existing Measures

How does the Graham et al. scale compare with those used in prior research? We chose two prominent scales to make comparisons, specifically using the traditional CTT metrics (i.e., factor loadings, Cronbach's α), IRT metrics (i.e., discrimination, difficulty, model fit, information, DIF), and predictive validity with police legitimacy, cooperation with police, and satisfaction with police. These comparisons are made possible by two sources of data. First, publicly accessible data permitted for direct examination of one of these scales, removing the limitation of item wording. Second, through virtue of returning to the first MTurk survey, which used a large pool of items to develop the Graham et al. scale, we can build many different scales from prior literature. Recall that this pool of items began with all items used to measure procedural justice in prior literature and was reduced by removing, for example, exact duplicates, similarly worded items, and double-barreled items. Therefore, we can identify items that were identical or nearly identical to the published scales for which we will compare to the Graham et al. scale.

As such, we first compare our 10-item scale with the measure of procedural justice contained in the 2010 European Social Survey (ESS), using the ESS publicly available data. This provides for a direct examination of the scale. However, as the name implies, it uses a European sample, so our US-developed Graham et al. scale may not be directly comparable. Therefore, we supplement this analysis with a second comparison of the ESS scale using items within our first MTurk survey from a US-based sample. This second comparison informs the sensitivity of the analyses conducted with the European sample. As reported in this section, the results of these two comparisons are similar.

The second measure chosen for comparison was authored by Sunshine and Tyler (2003a). It was the most frequently cited (i.e., used or adapted from) scale from the manuscripts in our systematic review. This comparative analysis must be considered only suggestive. As mentioned, our first MTurk survey did not contain an exact replica of the Sunshine and Tyler scale. However, we were able to select items that are worded almost identically to the items in their scale. We use this almost identically worded measure to undertake the comparison with our 10-item scale. As will be discussed, our almost identical scale performed similarly to the reported Sunshine and Tyler (2003a) scale, which bolsters our confidence in our findings. Additionally, the results are of value and illustrate how to conduct a comparison. Still, any findings reported should be more thoroughly examined through a direct replication using Sunshine and Tyler's (2003a) original scale.

We present a systematic comparison with our 10-item scale. Thus, for each scale, we make a total of 10 comparisons: (1) Cronbach's α, (2) factor loadings from an EFA, (3) convergent validity, (4) discriminant validity, (5) GRM difficulties, (6) GRM discriminations, (7) GRM model fit, (8) scale information, (9) DIF, and (10) predictive validity. We present the comparative Graham et al. scale statistics, using the MTurk 1 sample, in parentheses throughout this discussion for ease of comparison. Full statistical information on the Graham et al. scale from the MTurk 1 sample can be found in Section 4.

5.1.1 The European Social Survey

The ESS three-item scale was fielded within a nationally representative survey of 27 European countries in 2010 as part of a module on justice. This survey is conducted every two years to produce "cross-national data, in particular in regard to attitudes, beliefs, and values" (European Social Survey, 2024, p. 3). The items the ESS used to measure procedural justice in policing were:

1. Based on what you have heard or your own experience, how often would you say the police generally treat people in [country] with respect?
2. About how often would you say that the police make fair, impartial decisions in the cases they deal with?
3. And when dealing with people in [country], how often would you say the police generally explain their decisions and actions when asked to do so?

To assess and compare the ESS to the Graham et al. scale, we take two approaches (as noted earlier). First, we use the ESS 2010 data; this was when their "justice" module was fielded, which included these items. We analyze the scale by pooling all countries' data and engaging CTT and IRT analyses. However, these data were collected in 2010 and from a European sample. Comparisons made to our Graham et al. (2019) scale, derived from American samples nearly a decade later, thus may not offer the best comparison. As such, our second approach uses items from our first round of MTurk survey data. Again, although these items are not identical, they approximate the ESS items just listed.

We conduct nine comparisons, with the tenth not being readily comparable across the subsequent analyses due to missing predictors within the ESS dataset. Using a CTT approach, we make our first two comparisons. Analyses of the ESS 2010 data's scale demonstrate an adequate Cronbach's α (0.81; Graham et al. = 0.95) with acceptable factor loadings (between 0.68 and 0.83, $\bar{x}$ factor loadings = 0.77; Graham et al. = 0.73 to 0.86, $\bar{x}$ factor loadings = 0.82). For comparisons three and four, we assess the ESS 2010 scale's convergent validity (comparison #3), as

Table 16 Convergent and discriminant validity of ESS and Sunshine & Tyler (2003a) scales

		MTurk 1	
Correlations	**ESS 2010 Scale**	**ESS Scale**	**Sunshine & Tyler (2003a) Scale**
Age	0.080***	−0.048	−0.048
Education	−0.011*	0.073	0.095*
Income	–	0.090*	0.069
Politically right	0.067***	–	–
Support for government Intervention in income inequality	−0.117***	–	–
Immigration of other race/ ethnicity	0.071***	–	–
Safety walking alone at night	0.155***	–	–
Libertarianism	–	0.006	0.026
Racial resentment	–	0.179***	0.195***
Black Lives Matter support	–	−0.215***	−0.198***
Likely 2020 Trump voter	–	0.306***	0.330***
Police effectiveness	0.493***	0.794***	0.815***
Satisfaction with police	0.550***	0.755***	0.783***
Cooperation with police	–	0.593***	0.592***
Police legitimacy	0.212***	0.349***	0.367***
Law legitimacy	–	0.102**	0.113*

$^*p < 0.05$; $^{**}p < 0.01$; $^{***}p < 0.001$

seen in Table 16. The scale is significantly correlated with police effectiveness (r = 0.493; Graham et al. = 0.831; z = 14.33, $p < 0.001$), satisfaction ($r = 0.550$; Graham et al. = 0.779; z = 9.34, $p < 0.001$), and police legitimacy ($r = 0.212$; Graham et al. = 0.376; z = 3.96, $p < 0.001$). However, correlations were significantly smaller than the Graham et al. scale.

As for discriminant validity (comparisons #4), the ESS 2010 scale was significantly but weakly correlated with education ($r = -0.011$; Graham et al. = 0.065; z = 14.33, $p < 0.001$), age ($r = 0.080$; Graham et al. = −0.024; z = 1.19, $p = 0.234$), political leaning (right; r = 0.067), support for government intervention in addressing income disparities (r = −0.117), preferences for the number of individuals of other races/ethnicities (different from one's home country) allowed to immigrate (r = 0.071), and perceived safety when walking alone at night (r = 0.155). As such, this scale appears to have convergent and discriminant

Table 17 EFA of ESS and Sunshine & Tyler (2003a) scales with police legitimacy

			MTurk 1			
	ESS 2010 Scale		ESS Scale		Sunshine & Tyler (2003a) Scale	
	Factor 1	**Factor 2**	**Factor 1**	**Factor 2**	**Factor 1**	**Factor 2**
… the police generally treat people in [country] with respect?	0.660		–	–	–	–
… the police make fair, impartial decisions in the cases they deal with?	0.659		–	–	–	–
… how often would you say the police generally explain their decisions and actions when asked to do so?	0.480		–	–	–	–
… back the decisions made by the police even when you disagree with them?		0.683	–	–	–	–
… do what the police tell you even if you don't understand or agree with the reasons?		0.934	–	–	–	–
… do what the police tell you to do, even if you don't like how they treat you?		0.842	–	–	–	–
The police generally have the same sense of right and wrong as I do.	0.712		–	–	–	–

The police stand up for values that are important to people like me.	0.757		–	–	–	–
I generally support how the police usually act.	0.755		–	–	–	–
… usually treat people with respect.	–	–	0.479		–	–
… make decisions about what to do in fair ways.	–	–	0.504		0.814	
… explain their decisions.	–	–	0.499		–	–
… treat all people fairly	–	–	–	–	0.825	
… accurately understand the law	–	–	–	–	0.654	
… make their decisions based on facts	–	–	–	–	0.792	
… try to get the facts in a situation before deciding how to act	–	–	–	–	0.757	
… give honest explanations for their actions	–	–	–	–	0.868	
… apply the law consistently to everyone	–	–	–	–	0.751	
… consider people's views when deciding what to do	–	–	–	–	0.719	
… take people's needs into consideration	–	–	–	–	0.785	
… treat everyone with dignity	–	–	–	–	0.845	
… treat everyone with respect	–	–	–	–	0.850	
… respect people's rights	–	–	–	–	0.773	
	–	–	0.492			0.576

Table 17 (cont.)

			MTurk 1			
	ESS 2010 Scale		ESS Scale		Sunshine & Tyler (2003a) Scale	
	Factor 1	**Factor 2**	**Factor 1**	**Factor 2**	**Factor 1**	**Factor 2**
You should support the decisions made by police even when you disagree.						
You should do what the police tell you even if you do not agree.	–	–		0.944		0.656
The police in your community are legitimate authorities.	–	–		0.817		0.756
You should do what the police tell you to do even if you do not like how they treat you	–	–		0.908		0.679
The police stand up for values that are important to you.	–	–	0.465	0.766		0.828
You generally support how the police act in your community.	–	–	0.525	0.729		0.861
The police act in ways consistent with your own ideas of right and wrong.	–	–	0.480	0.787		0.855
Percent variation	32.3	24.5	30.8	28.2	40.8	22.3

Note: Promax rotation; only loadings > 0.400 are displayed.

validity. Still, an additional check on the discriminant validity of this scale was conducted, placing the procedural justice items into the same EFA as items used to measure police legitimacy. As seen in Table 17, three police legitimacy items loaded highly on the same factor as the three items used to construct procedural justice. As such, the discriminant validity of the ESS 2010 scale is wanting.

We then examine these data and scale using IRT techniques, which produce statistics for our remaining five comparisons. The scale's threshold difficulties (comparison #5) ranged from −1.987 to 1.786 (Graham et al. = −2.468 to 0.877) and held discrimination values (comparisons #6; see Table 18) that are deemed acceptable but are lower than most items in the Graham et al. scale (2.465 to 4.315; ESS $\bar{x}$ discrimination = 2.951; Graham et al. $\bar{x}$ discrimination = 3.371). Examination of the model fit (comparison #7; see RMSEA) finds that the GRM for these data fits within accepted standards. However, the scale's information (comparison #8; the scale's ability to precisely measure an individual's level of procedural justice) does not have adequate information at any point in the scale (see Figure 10). As such, the scale cannot precisely measure levels of perceived procedural justice.

Recall that we want scales that can precisely place respondents on the scale of procedural justice (and other constructs, respectively). This evidence suggests that the ESS scale cannot achieve this goal. This may be a function of the scale's brevity, but longer scales are not necessarily more valid or reliable (Niemi et al., 1986). However, examination of the items' DIF (whether or not an item has invariance between groups; comparison #9) across gender, age (split at the median), and education (split at the median) finds that all three items exhibit DIF across all three characteristics.

As a check on the sensitivity of these findings, we analyze three similarly worded items found in our first round of MTurk survey data that are comparable to the ESS in emphasizing respect, fairness, and explanation. Again, the survey was conducted with a 2019 American sample. These items were: The police in my community (1) usually treat people with respect, (2) make decisions about what to do in fair ways, and (3) explain their decisions. We calculated that the MTurk ESS scale had a Cronbach's α of 0.84 (comparison #1; Graham et al. = 0.95) and acceptable factor loadings (between 0.78 and 0.83, $\bar{x}$ factor loadings = 0.80; comparisons #2; Graham et al. = 0.734 to 0.864, $\bar{x}$ factor loadings = 0.82). Compared to our 10-item scale, the MTurk ESS scale produced a lower Cronbach's α but roughly similar factor loadings. This may be a function of the brevity of the ESS scale and how Cronbach's α is computed – longer scales tend to have higher α's. As seen in Table 16, the convergent and discriminant validity of the MTurk ESS scale was examined. These analyses found significant correlations with police effectiveness (r = 0.794; Graham et al. = 0.831; z = 1.71,

Table 18 ESS and MTurk ESS item discriminations and differential item functioning

Items	Discrimination	RMSEA (CI)	Differential item functioning		
ESS 2010	**N = 41,421**		**Gender**	**Age (split at median = 47)**	**Education (split at median = 4)**
1. Based on what you have heard or your own experience, how often would you say the police generally treat people in [country] with respect?	3.111		X	X	X
2. About how often would you say that the police make fair, impartial decisions in the cases they deal with?	3.721		X	X	X
3. And when dealing with people in [country], how often would you say the police generally explain their decisions and actions when asked to do so?	2.022		X	X	X
		0.044 (0.043– 0.046)			

MTurk 1	N = 493			(split at 34)	(split at 5)
"The police in my community … "					
1. Usually treat people with respect.	2.860		X	–	–
2. Explain their decisions.	2.851		X	–	X
3. Make decisions about what to do in fair ways.	3.319		X	–	X
		0.060 (0.048–0.072)			

Note: X indicates significant differential item functioning between groups.

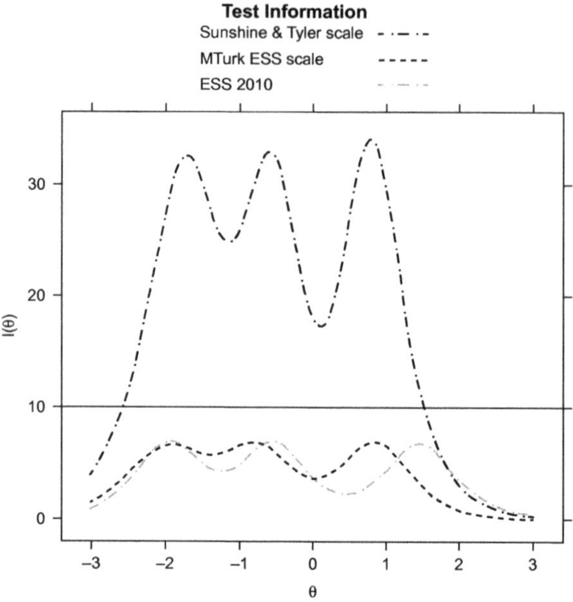

Figure 10 Test information of ESS 2010, MTurk ESS, and Sunshine & Tyler (2003a) scales.

$p = 0.087$), satisfaction ($r = 0.755$; Graham et al. = 0.779; z = 0.91, $p = 0.361$), cooperation ($r = 0.593$; Graham et al. = 0.624; z = 0.77, $p = 0.441$), police legitimacy ($r = 0.349$; Graham et al. = 0.376; z = 0.49, $p = 0.627$), and law legitimacy ($r = 0.102$; Graham et al. = 0.116; z = 22, $p = 0.825$). Furthermore, the scale was weakly or not significantly correlated with education ($r = 0.073$; Graham et al. = 0.065; z = 0.13, $p = 0.900$), age ($r = -0.048$; Graham et al. = −0.024; z = 0.38, $p = 0.707$), income ($r = 0.090$; Graham et al. = 0.077; z = 0.20, $p = 0.838$), or libertarianism ($r = 0.006$; Graham et al. = 0.021; z = 0.23, $p = 0.814$) and was significantly, but weakly, correlated with racial resentment ($r = 0.179$; Graham et al. = 0.167; z = 0.19, $p = 0.847$), support for Black Lives Matter ($r = -0.215$; Graham et al. = −0.191; z = 0.39, $p = 0.695$), and 2020 likely vote choice (Trump; $r = 0.306$; Graham et al. = 0.282; z = 0.41, $p = 0.681$).

Additionally, the items used to construct this measure of procedural justice were placed in the same EFA as police legitimacy items, finding that four of the police legitimacy items loaded on the same factor as items used to construct the measure of procedural justice (see Table 17). As such, these analyses demonstrate convergent (comparison #3), but discriminant validity is wanting (comparison #4) for the ESS MTurk scale.

When subjected to IRT methods (GRM), the MTurk ESS scale threshold difficulties (comparison #5) ranged from −2.314 to 0.906, which is similar to our scale (−2.468 to 0.877). However, the MTurk ESS scale item discriminations (comparison #6), seen in Table 18, were generally lower (though still acceptable) compared to many items used in the Graham et al. scale (2.465 to 4.315). The model's RMSEA is 0.06 (comparison #7; Graham et al. = 0.020, CI = 0–0.049), which falls outside of the needed threshold to demonstrate close model fit (Steiger, 1990). Furthermore, an examination of the scale's information plot in Figure 10 (comparison #8) finds that, along θ, this scale's information never reaches the adequacy threshold of 10 (Brown, 2018). In short, the items used in this scale do not have enough information to precisely and reliably locate individuals along the continuum of θ (procedural justice). Examination of items' DIF across gender, age, and education (comparison #9) finds DIF for all items with gender, no DIF for age, and DIF for two of the three items for education.

Finally, for comparison #10, as a check on the predictive validity of this scale, it was used as a predictor in three OLS regression models, predicting the theoretical outcomes of police legitimacy, cooperation with police, and satisfaction with police. As seen in Table 19, the ESS MTurk scale was significantly associated with each outcome. As such, the scale can be said to exhibit predictive validity.

In sum, what do these two comparisons tell us about the merits of the ESS's scale for procedural justice? By CTT standards, the ESS scale, as examined by their 2010 data or our MTurk data, appears to perform within recommended standards, except for discriminant validity, which produced mixed evidence.

By IRT standards, the ESS items demonstrate acceptable discriminations and a similar range of difficulties as the Graham et al. scale. However, the GRM fit statistics show superior functioning for the Graham et al. scale. For the ESS scale, the RMSEA falls outside accepted thresholds, which can provide misleading inferences (Maydeu-Olivares, 2015). The most problematic result concerning the ESS scale's capacity is its lack of precision and DIF. Because the ESS scale's information never exceeds 10, the accepted threshold for scale precision in the IRT framework (Brown, 2018), it cannot reliably or accurately locate an individual's level of perceived procedural justice along the continuum of this latent trait. Furthermore, in both the ESS 2010 and our MTurk data, this scale exhibited DIF across three common sociodemographic characteristics. Ultimately, given the evidence just reported, the Graham et al. scale is to be preferred over the ESS scale as it matches the strengths of the ESS scale and performs substantially better in its capacity to locate respondents on a continuous dimension of procedural justice.

Table 19 OLS regression models – MTurk 1 sample

	ESS MTurk 1									Sunshine & Tyler (2003a)								
	Legitimacy (N = 493)			Cooperation (N = 493)			Satisfaction (N = 493)			Legitimacy (N = 493)			Cooperation (N = 493)			Satisfaction (N = 493)		
	b	SE	β	b	SE	β	b	SE	β	b	SE	β	b	SE	β	b	SE	β
Procedural justice	0.421	0.051	0.364***	0.341	0.025	0.533***	0.715	0.033	0.713***	0.415	0.047	0.385***	0.321	0.024	0.539***	0.702	0.029	0.752***
Contacted police (Y)	−0.133	0.107	−0.060	0.101	0.050	0.082*	−0.068	0.064	−0.035	−0.134	0.106	−0.060	0.107	0.050	0.087*	−0.067	0.061	−0.035
Stopped by police (Y)	0.030	0.105	0.013	−0.053	0.049	−0.041	0.121	0.063	0.060	0.026	0.104	0.011	−0.059	0.049	−0.046	0.113	0.060	0.056
Age	0.007	0.105	0.067	0.004	0.002	0.071	−0.001	0.003	−0.005	0.007	0.005	0.067	0.004	0.002	0.070	−0.000	0.003	−0.004
Male	−0.029	0.094	−0.014	−0.068	0.044	−0.057	−0.066	0.056	−0.035	−0.040	0.093	−0.019	−0.081	0.044	−0.067	−0.088	0.053	−0.047
White	−0.071	0.110	−0.027	0.072	0.052	0.050	−0.076	0.066	−0.034	−0.068	0.110	−0.026	0.075	0.051	0.052	−0.072	0.063	−0.032
Education	−0.033	0.036	−0.041	0.002	0.017	0.004	0.019	0.022	0.027	−0.041	0.036	−0.051	−0.004	0.017	−0.009	0.006	0.021	0.008
Income	0.011	0.032	0.016	0.038	0.015	0.095*	0.010	0.019	0.016	0.018	0.032	0.025	0.045	0.015	0.111**	0.022	0.018	0.035
Conservativism	−0.011	0.056	−0.009	−0.026	0.026	−0.037	−0.020	0.033	−0.019	0.008	0.055	0.006	−0.013	0.026	−0.018	0.011	0.032	0.010
Legitimacy	–	–	–	0.037	0.021	0.068	0.100	0.027	0.116***	–	–	–	0.030	0.021	0.055	0.076	0.026	0.087**
Intercept	3.304	0.313	–	2.788	0.162	–	3.496	0.207	–	3.275	0.310	–	2.792	0.162	–	3.529	0.197	–
Adjusted R-squared		0.116			0.374			0.581			0.131			0.375			0.620	

$^{*}p < 0.05$; $^{**}p < 0.01$; $^{***}p < 0.001$

5.1.2 Sunshine and Tyler (2003a)

The second scale we used for comparison purposes is Sunshine and Tyler's (2003a) scale. In the systematic review of the literature we conducted, this measure was used at least 16 times – the most frequently reported of any procedural justice scale. Sunshine and Tyler's (2003a) measure consisted of 11 items:

How frequently do police:[32]

1. Make decisions about how to handle problems in fair ways.
2. Treat people fairly.

Do police:

3. Usually accurately understand and apply the law.
4. Make their decisions based upon facts, not their personal biases or opinions.
5. Try to get the facts in a situation before deciding how to act.
6. Give honest explanations for their actions to the people they deal with.
7. Apply the rules consistently to different people.
8. Consider the views of the people involved when deciding what to do.
9. Take account of the needs and concerns of the people they deal with.
10. Treat people with dignity and respect.
11. Respect people's rights.

Items 1, 5, 6, 9, 10, and 11 are similar to items in the newly developed Graham et al. scale.[33] For example, Sunshine & Tyler's (2003a) first item is similar to the Graham et al. ninth item ("make decisions about what to do in fair ways"). Likewise, Sunshine and Tyler's (2003a) last item is similar to Graham et al.'s "respect your basic rights" (item 4). Although these items likely tap into similar ideas, the slight variation in language may produce different effects in the measurement of procedural justice.

As noted, the first MTurk survey did not contain the exact wording of the items used by Sunshine and Tyler (2003a). However, our survey did include items that approximated their measure, which were selected to create a close proxy for their scale. For example, "treat all people fairly" was used in place of

[32] Note that Sunshine and Tyler (2003a) do not provide the exact question stem wording for their items. The stems provided here are derived from their discussion of these items within their Appendix B.

[33] Item wording between MTurk 1 data and Sunshine and Tyler (2003a) varied slightly. See Table 18 for details.

Sunshine and Tyler's (2003a) "treat people fairly." Likewise, "accurately understand the law" was used in place of Sunshine and Tyler's (2003a) "usually accurately understand and apply the law." Again, these items are not *exactly* the wording used by Sunshine and Tyler (2003a), but they serve as a close proxy for their measure. Conclusions about the Sunshine and Tyler (2003a) scale should be viewed in this light. In full, the scale used for comparison used the following items:

The police in my community …

1. Make decisions about how to handle problems in fair ways.
2. Treat all people fairly.
3. Accurately understand the law.
4. Make their decisions based on facts.
5. Try to get the facts in a situation before deciding how to act.
6. Give honest explanations for their actions.
7. Apply the law consistently to everyone.
8. Consider people's views when deciding what to do.
9. Take people's needs into consideration.
10. a. Treat everyone with dignity.
10. b. Treat everyone with respect.
11. Respect people's rights.

Using data from the first MTurk survey, we find the Sunshine and Tyler (2003a) scale has a Cronbach's α of 0.96 (comparison #1; Graham et al. = 0.95) and factor loadings between 0.68 and 0.88, with mean factor loadings of 0.82 (comparison #2; Graham et al. = 0.734 to 0.864, $\bar{x}$ factor loadings = 0.82), which are respectable within the CTT framework. Additionally, Sunshine & Tyler's (2003a) manuscript reports a comparable α of 0.98, bolstering our confidence that our Sunshine & Tyler (2003a) scale is similar to that of the published scale. Nonetheless, the Graham et al. scale provides similar α's but higher factor loadings (the lowest factor loading was 0.770) when using the first MTurk survey data. In these data, Sunshine and Tyler's (2003a) scale was weakly or not significantly correlated with education (r = 0.095; Graham et al. = 0.065; z = 0.47, p = 0.637), age (r = −0.048; Graham et al. = −0.024; z = 0.38, p = 0.707), or income (r = 0.069; Graham et al. = 0.077; z = 0.13, p = 0.900), and was significantly, but weakly, correlated with racial resentment (r = 0.195; Graham et al. = 0.167; z = 0.45, p = 0.650), support for Black Lives Matter (r = −0.198; Graham et al. = −0.191; z = 1.78, p = 0.075), and 2020 likely vote choice (Trump; r = 0.330; Graham et al. = 0.282; z = 0.83, p = 0.407).

Similar to the Graham et al. scale, it was significantly correlated with police effectiveness (r = 0.815; Graham et al. = 0.831; z = 0.78, p = 0.437), satisfaction

($r = 0.783$; Graham et al. = 0.779; z = 0.16, $p = 0.873$), cooperation ($r = 0.592$; Graham et al. = 0.624; z = 0.80, $p = 0.427$), police legitimacy ($r = 0.367$; Graham et al. = 0.376; z = 0.16, $p = 0.870$), and law legitimacy ($r = 0.113$; Graham et al. = 0.116; z = 0.05, $p = 0.962$), thus demonstrating convergent (comparison #3) and discriminant validity (see Table 16; comparison #4).

As an additional check on the discriminant validity, the Sunshine and Tyler (2003a) scale was subjected to an EFA that included items used to measure police legitimacy. As seen in Table 17, the procedural justice and police legitimacy items loaded highly onto their independent respective factors. This also bolsters claims of discriminant validity for the Sunshine and Tyle (2003a) scale.

Under the IRT framework (using a GRM), the Sunshine and Tyler (2003a) scale threshold difficulties range between −2.418 and 1.255 (comparison #5; Graham et al. = −2.468 to 0.877), and discriminations range between 2.051 and 4.499 (comparison #6; Graham et al. = 2.465 to 4.315) – both slightly wider than the Graham et al. 10-item scale (see Tables 9 and 20). This GRM model-fit statistic for Sunshine and Tyler's (2003a) scale provided indications of poorer fit (RMSEA = 0.064, CFI = 0.969, TLI = 0.956, SRMSR = 0.033) than the Graham et al. scale (comparison #7; RMSEA = 0.020, CFI = 0.995; TLI = 0.997; SRMSR = 0.023), but the scale had adequate information (< 10) across the span of θ (see Figure 10; comparison #8). In contrast, the GRM model-fit for our 10-item scale exceeded the standards for adequate fit across all metrics (Table 11). Examination of the items' DIF across gender, age, and education (comparison #9) finds DIF with 3 items for gender, 0 items for age, and 7 items for education.

Finally, for the tenth comparison, the predictive validity of the Sunshine and Tyler (2003a) scale was examined through three OLS regression models, predicting theoretical outcomes of procedural justice. As seen in Table 19, the Sunshine and Tyler (2003a) scale is significantly associated with the three theoretical outcomes. As such, the scale can be said to have predictive validity. Given slight tweaks to the Sunshine and Tyler (2003a) scale to improve its model fit, such as removing items with lower factor loadings or discrimination, this scale may be a suitable alternative to our Graham et al. scale.

What does this tell us about the Sunshine and Tyler (2003a) scale? Based on CTT metrics, Sunshine and Tyler's (2003a) 11-item scale meets the expected standards and appears comparable to the Graham et al. scale. Under IRT standards, the Sunshine and Tyler (2003a) scale has adequate discriminations and a similar range of difficulties to the Graham et al. scale. However, the point estimate of the RMSEA for the model fit (0.063) exceeds the recommended levels (0.05), which might

Table 20 Sunshine and Tyler (2003a)* Item discriminations and differential item functioning

Items	MTurk 1 N = 493	Differential item functioning: Gender	Age (split at median)	Education (split at median)
The police in my community …				
1. Make decisions about how to handle problems in fair ways.	3.555	X	–	X
2. Treat all people fairly.	3.925	–	–	X
3. Accurately understand the law.	2.051	X	–	X
4. Make their decisions based on facts.	3.084	–	–	–
5. Try to get the facts in a situation before deciding how to act.	2.785	–	–	X
6. Give honest explanations for their actions.	4.499	–	–	–
7. Apply the law consistently to everyone.	2.695	–	–	X
8. Consider people's views when deciding what to do.	2.280	–	–	X
9. Take people's needs into consideration.	3.023	–	–	–
10a. Treat everyone with dignity.	4.235	–	–	–
10b. Treat everyone with respect.	4.361	X	–	X
11. Respect people's rights.	3.001	–	–	–
Model fit				
RMSEA (CI)	0.064 (0.049–0.079)			
CFI/TLI	0.969/0.956			
SRMSR	0.033			

* **Note:** MTurk and Sunshine & Tyler's (2003a) word choice varied for the following items (item wording used in parentheses): 2 (treat all people fairly), 3 (accurately understand the law), 4 (make decisions based on facts), 6 (give honest explanations for their actions), 7 (apply the law consistently to everyone), 8 (consider people's views when deciding what to do), 9 (take people's needs into consideration), 10 (treat everyone with dignity; treat everyone with respect; treated as two questions because originally double-barreled); X indicates significant DIF between groups.

lead to biased inferences (Maydeu-Olivares, 2015). However, the RMSEA confidence interval does include the 0.05 threshold. Nonetheless, to its credit, the Sunshine and Tyler (2003a) scale has enough information across the continuum of the latent construct to reliably and precisely measure respondents' levels of perceived procedural justice. The Sunshine and Tyler (2003a) scale also exhibited some DIF, particularly for education, but none for age and very little for gender.

5.2 The Final Adjudication

Table 21 provides an overarching summary of these comparisons, with the recommended thresholds for adequacy in parentheses. All three comparison scales (ESS 2010, MTurk ESS, and Sunshine & Tyler) have adequate Cronbach's α and factor loadings, based on expected standards within the field. All three also exhibited convergent and discriminant validity – strongly correlating with related constructs and weakly correlating with unrelated constructs, respectively. However, the ESS scale did not exhibit discriminant validity when subjected to an EFA with police legitimacy items. Furthermore, all provided evidence of predictive validity with theoretical outcomes.[34] Based on CTT metrics alone, one might be tempted to argue that at least two of the three are valid and reliable scales, worthy of use. However, IRT metrics expose the flaws within these scales.

The three-item ESS scales (2010 and MTurk) never achieve information greater than 10, suggesting a lack of precision in estimates. Likewise, the MTurk ESS scale suffers from inadequate model fit, which could bias inferences made with this scale, including increased Type I or II errors. For example, Hu and Bentler (1999) find that misfitting models using a cutoff for their RMSEA of 0.06 exhibit between 8.2 percent Type II error (with simple models and large (N > 1,000) samples) and 100 percent Type II error (with complex models and small (N < 250) samples). Model fit for the 2010 ESS scale is likely aided by the large sample size (N = 40,586), but Hu and Bentler (1999) warn that it may still include 5.4 percent Type I error. Furthermore, both ESS scales suffer from DIF, with items performing differently between men and women as well as between those with higher and lower levels of education.

[34] Although each scale operated similarly when examining predictive validity, it is important to note that the procedural justice coefficients for each scale were statistically similar in the legitimacy models (based on an equality of coefficients test; Paternoster et al., 1998). However, coefficients for the ESS and Sunshine and Tyler scales were significantly larger than the Graham et al. scale in the cooperation and satisfaction models, suggesting overestimated effects of procedural justice with these two outcomes when using the ESS and Sunshine and Tyler scales.

Table 21 Summary of comparisons

Statistics	Scales			
	Graham et al. (MTurk 1)	**ESS 2010**	**ESS MTurk**	**Sunshine & Tyler**
Classical test theory (CTT)				
1. Cronbach's α (> 0.70)	0.95	0.81	0.84	0.96
2. Factor loading range (> 0.40)	0.73 to 0.86	0.68 to 0.83	0.78 to 0.83	0.68 to 0.88
3. Convergent validity	Yes	Yes	Yes	Yes
4. Discriminant validity				
4a. Correlations	Yes	Yes	Yes	Yes
4b. EFA with Legitimacy	Yes	No – cross-loading items	No – cross-loading items	Yes
Item response theory (IRT)				
5. Threshold difficulty range (−3 to 3)	−2.468 to 0.877	−1.987 to 1.786	−2.314 to 0.906	−2.418 to 1.255
6. Discrimination range (> 1.70)	2.465 to 4.315	2.022 to 3.721	2.851 to 3.319	2.051 to 4.499
7. IRT model fit: RMSEA (CI) (< 0.05)	0.020 (0 to 0.049)	0.044 (0.043 to 0.046)	0.060 (0.048 to 0.072)	0.064 (0.049 to 0.079)

8. Information > 10?	Yes	No	No	Yes
9. Differential item functioning				
9a. Gender	Yes (minor)	Yes	Yes	Yes (minor)
9b. Age	Yes	Yes	No	No
9c. Education	No	Yes	Yes	Yes
10. Predictive validity (legitimacy; cooperation; satisfaction)*				
10a. Procedural justice β	0.387; 0.575; 0.742	–	0.364; 0.533; 0.713	0.385; 0.539; 0.752
10b. Model adjusted R-squared	0.136; 0.412; 0.616	–	0.116; 0.374; 0.581	0.131; 0.375; 0.620

* **Note:** All analyses for the predictive validity were conducted using the MTurk 1 sample so that comparisons across scales could be made more equivalent.

Moving on, the Sunshine and Tyler (2003a) scale performs better than either of the ESS scales under IRT metrics. It has information greater than 10, which indicates precision in measurement, and has less DIF than the ESS scales. One might be tempted to argue that this is simply a reflection of a longer scale, but a longer scale does not inherently produce a more valid or reliable scale (Neimi et al., 1986). Additionally, simulation-based studies have demonstrated that even short scales (containing as few as three items) can meet the information threshold required, contingent on high discriminating items and sufficient sample size (Dai et al., 2021).

However, it too has flaws in model fit. The Sunshine and Tyler (2003a) scale's RMSEA falls outside of the recommended threshold, suggesting inferences made may be biased, increasing the risk for Type I and II errors. Still, the Sunshine and Tyler (2003a) scale is formidable and preferable to the 2010 and MTurk ESS scales. But we temper these conclusions by the fact that we could only examine this scale using items that closely proxied the Sunshine and Tyler (2003a) scale, not the same items or question stem. Thus, future research should examine this scale using the exact question stem and items to understand the limitations of our conclusions.

Continuing, the Graham et al. scale performs the same or better than both the ESS scale and the Sunshine and Tyler (2003a) scale across both CTT and IRT metrics. It meets all CTT metric standards. Likewise, it meets IRT standards for discrimination, information, and model fit. In fact, concerning IRT model fit, it is nearly significantly better than the ESS and Sunshine and Tyler (2003a) scales – the model RMSEA confidence intervals barely overlap, and the Graham et al. scale point estimate falls outside of the ESS and Sunshine and Tyler (2003a) scale RMSEA confidence intervals.

Notably, as seen in Table 21, the Graham et al. scale explains more variance than the ESS scale and Sunshine and Tyler (2003a) scale. Using the MTurk 1 sample to make more equivalent comparisons between scales, the Graham et al. scale was subjected to the same three OLS regression models as the ESS MTurk and Sunshine and Tyler (2003a) scales, using the same covariates and outcomes. As a result, differences between model R-squared values reflect the procedural justice scale used within the model. As seen in Table 21, the Graham et al. scale models explain more variance than the ESS MTurk models (0.136 vs. 0.116; 0.412 vs. 0.375; 0.616 vs. 0.581, respectively). Likewise, the Sunshine and Tyler (2003a) scale models explain more than the ESS scale models (0.116 vs. 0.131; 0.374 vs. 0.375; 0.581 vs. 0.620, respectively).

Additionally, the Graham et al. scale models explain more variance than the Sunshine and Tyler (2003a) models for two of the three models (0.136 vs. 0.131; 0.412 vs. 0.375, respectively); the third (satisfaction with police) falls only shortly behind (0.616 vs. 0.620). Given that the popularly used Sunshine and Tyler (2003a) scale was rooted in theory and contained items to capture Tyler's (2000) four key elements, it was a strong contender for comparisons with the Graham et al. scale. And, although the Sunshine and Tyler (2003a) scale captures more variance in one of the three models, a looming question remains. Does the Sunshine and Tyler (2003a) scale account for the appropriate unique variance in the outcome that should be attributed to procedural justice or not? It is possible that the Sunshine and Tyler (2003a) scale, which shared only one of the same items as the Graham et al. scale (scale $r = 0.947$), may have captured variance that should be assigned to a related construct, such as legitimacy or prior expectations, which are either unmeasured (i.e., not included in the model) or poorly measured (i.e., not criminometrically developed). Without additional measures being crimnometrically derived, it is impossible to answer this question. Nevertheless, the Graham et al. scale outperforms the Sunshine and Tyler (2003a) scale in two of the three models, suggesting it is slightly better than Sunshine and Tyler's scale. Based on this overall assessment, the Graham et al. scale performs better than the ESS and Sunshine and Tyler (2003a) scales.

5.3 Conclusion

This section sought to answer whether the Graham et al. scale, developed with modern psychometric methods within this Element, performed the same or better than existing scales of procedural justice. The answer: It performed similarly, if not better.

This is not to say that our scale is the *best* measure to *ever* measure procedural justice in policing; improvements can be made. Rather, compared to two existing measures, our scale performed similarly, if not better, across all CTT and IRT metrics. Furthermore, we have only compared our scale to two (of many) possible scales used in published research on procedural justice in policing. However, our Graham et al. scale now serves a key purpose: It is a benchmark by which other measures of procedural justice (old and new) can be compared and evaluated. In Section 6, we will expand on these implications for policing and criminology.

6 The Future of Measurement: Criminometrics as a Research Paradigm

This Element has illuminated a hidden crisis of measurement within criminology – the failure of scholars to use modern psychometric methods to measure key concepts. The goal has been to provide a feasible solution to this crisis by articulating a road map to create better measures. Concretely, a case study was undertaken to produce a new measure of procedural justice in policing, the Graham et al. scale. This effort was intended to furnish a template in psychometric methods to develop measures of all major concepts. In short, this Element calls for a turning point in criminology by creating its own novel methodological subfield of "criminometrics." In this section, we discuss this path forward.

6.1 Doing Better Criminology: Why Now?

As mentioned in Section 2, psychology has long prioritized the measurement of concepts. Albeit, best practices are not always followed. Still, within psychology, there is a recognition of the steps to construct quality measures. We advocate the systematic application of principles developed under the rubric of psychometrics in psychology to the conceptualization and measurement of key constructs in criminology. We call this *criminometrics*.

Nonetheless, this emphasis and the advancement of psychology's psychometric science has not been fortuitous nor foreordained. Rather, it was (and continues to be) a concerted effort by multiple individuals over several decades who pursued the goal of improved measurement to understand psychology. Psychology's emphasis on psychometrics dates back to Francis Galton's 1879 publication in *Brain*, "Psychometric Experiments." Galton, the half cousin of Charles Darwin, was enamored with Darwin's *The Origin of Species*, particularly the potential for and measurement of variation in humans (Fancher, 1998). It is Galton's work that influenced James Cattell, a student of Wilhelm Wundt (the father of experimental psychology), to combine individual differences with statistical measurement, developing "mental tests" to measure intelligence and other basic human senses (Cattell, 1890; Hunt, 1936).

Psychometrics eventually gained traction as a subfield of psychology in 1935 through the development of the Psychometric Society and its peer-reviewed journal, *Psychometrika* (Springer, 2024). The founders of this society convened, not to necessarily start a society, but to start a journal dedicated to quantitative methods "as applied to education and psychology" (Psychometric Society, n.d.). Today, this journal, *Psychometrika*, is "devoted to the development of psychology as a quantitative rational science," which examines "statistical methods, discuss[es] mathematical techniques, and advance[s] theory for evaluating behavioral data in psychology, education, and the social and behavioral sciences generally" (Springer, 2024).

Why does this matter for criminology and criminologists? In short, the tale of psychology and psychometrics should serve as a road map guiding the future of criminometrics. But why now? Thelma Hunt's (1936) recounting of the history of psychometrics provides some insight. She states: "Except for some few instances of purely accidental discovery, applied fields of a science are developed only when (1) attitudes both of the scientists and of the public are conducive to the development, (2) needs for the application exist, and (3) techniques in the new science have been refined sufficiently to make the new application possible from a technical standpoint" (Hunt, 1936, p. 24). Criminology is rife with scholars calling for better measurement of constructs and improved theories (see, e.g., Armstrong et al., 2009; Bernard, 1990; Burt, 2019; Cullen et al., 2019a, 2019b; Gau, 2011, 2014; Gomes et al., 2019; Grasmick et al., 1993; Higgins, 2007; Mazerolle, Bennett, et al., 2013; Osgood et al., 2002; Piquero et al., 2000; Pratt, 2015; Reisig et al., 2007; Weisburd & Piquero, 2008; Wikström & Kroneberg, 2022). Furthermore, the public views crime and violence as some of their top concerns (Pew Research Center, 2024), which our field's research might seek to address. Attitudes appear conducive.

Likewise, the need for better measures exists for theoretical testing and aiding in solving practical problems (e.g., poor police–community relations). For example, without an accurate measure of procedural justice in policing, how do we know if reform efforts aimed at improving perceptions of procedural justice work? A *need* for criminometrics is apparent. Finally, technological (e.g., computers, online opt-in surveys) and statistical (e.g., IRT) advancements have made the technical aspects of robust measurement easier and cheaper than ever. The technical means for criminometrics exist. In short, Hunt's (1936) criteria for developing a field of science lead us to conclude that criminometrics should be born – now.

6.2 Implications of the Graham et al. Scale

This study sought to advance the measurement of procedural justice following the psychometric steps of construct development laid out by psychology. This approach involved defining the construct, developing a pool of items, pilot testing these items, analyzing their properties using CTT and IRT, narrowing this pool of items, retesting and analyzing these items (twice), and producing a scale with validated properties for measuring procedural justice in the context of policing. The Graham et al. scale most closely reflects Tyler and Blader's (2000) two-component model of procedural justice and Tyler's (2000) four key elements of procedural justice. This Element is part of the final step – documenting the scale, properties, and use (AERA et al., 2014).

The Graham et al. scale developed here is only the first of hopefully many future criminometrically developed constructs. Given its construction, several implications merit discussion. We start by discussing the scale's importance for policing and procedural justice before considering the broader implications for the field of criminology. We close this Element, noting the limitations of our current scale and proposing avenues for future efforts.

6.2.1 Implications for Policing and Procedural Justice

The analyses suggest that this scale has robust psychometric properties and thus can be used in research aimed at building a more cohesive understanding of procedural justice in the context of the process-based model of policing. Going forward, we thus propose that the Graham et al. scale should be used by policing scholars in studies seeking to advance the science of policing and police–community relations by investigating the impact of procedural justice. Clear next steps for the process-based model of policing are to develop psychometrically derived measures of police legitimacy, law legitimacy, cooperation with police, compliance with police, satisfaction with police, moral alignment with the police, and other variables. The utility of an entire psychometrically sound process-based model of policing cannot be understated, especially if it aims to decrease crime while building trust in the police (President's Task Force on 21st Century Policing, 2015; Tyler & Nobo, 2022). Reducing the measurement error that currently exists in extant empirical evaluations of this model of policing will provide a more falsifiable test of this model for procedural justice policing reform proponents and opponents alike.

Furthermore, for police researchers and practitioners, the repeated use of high-quality scales, such as the Graham et al. scale, provides the capacity to evaluate a police department's performance. Are the police perceived as procedurally fair? Or, is there room for improvement? Have perceptions of fairness increased or decreased over time? Are there geographic areas within a community that have distinctly different views about the procedural fairness of a department? How does one department stack up against another regarding their perceived procedural fairness within their communities? Did a police department's program or training influence community perceptions of procedural justice (e.g., Canales et al., 2020; Wood et al., 2020)? These questions could be addressed through this scale's consistent and repeated use.

In addition, the comparisons made between our scale and the ESS and Sunshine and Tyler (2003a) scales provide evidence for the utility of developing scales with psychometric methods, specifically in three ways. First, as seen in the example of the ESS scale, using specific items matters, particularly in shorter scales, to produce robust, precise, and reliable measures. No matter the size of their sample, this scale will still struggle with precision in measurement across the continuum of the construct. However, the Sunshine and Tyler (2003a) scale performed admirably, particularly for a scale that was not systematically developed.

Despite sharing items similar to our Graham et al. scale, the Sunshine and Tyler (2003a) scale still has weaknesses. This is the high cost of using unsystematically developed or ad hoc measures. As such, these comparisons to our scale emphasize the need to use a systematic criminometric approach to scale development. Without such an approach, researchers are left with the complete discretion to use any scale, with any number of items and response options, which undoubtedly compounds the issue of measurement heterogeneity. Furthermore, researchers end up relying on chance that their items produce a scale with high validity and reliability. However, measures built using psychometric principles will address measurement heterogeneity and lend legitimacy to the research and researchers who use them.

Second, comparisons made with our scale demonstrate that classically acceptable CTT metrics do not tell us all we need to know; principles of IRT are needed to understand the strengths and weaknesses of our measures. In the case of the Sunshine and Tyler (2003a) scale, only minor changes would likely be needed to produce a close-fitting model with higher discriminations. Under CTT, making these small adjustments is challenging because CTT metrics examine the test as a whole. The utility of IRT is its ability to show which items in the analysis might help the researcher achieve their measurement goals, be it increasing the difficulty, producing a scale that is reliable across the span of the construct (e.g., test information), or shortening a scale but retaining its strong measurement properties.

Third, our scale can be used as a benchmark for evaluating the utility of extant and new measures of procedural justice, as exemplified by the comparisons we highlighted between Graham et al. and ESS and Sunshine and Tyler. Arguably, under the scrutiny of IRT metrics, our scale performed much better than the ESS scale, having adequate information to measure procedural justice reliably and less DIF. Likewise, our scale performed better than Sunshine & Tyler's (2003a) scale, in model fit, which plays a role in producing reliable inferences about procedural justice. In making these comparisons, the field can reduce the measurement heterogeneity of procedural justice by pitting measures against each other and providing evidence that a measure meets or exceeds the current standards, lest it be discarded or replaced with a better-performing measure. Such methods outlined in this Element provide a path for which measures can be vetted more empirically to contribute to knowledge growth.

Fourth, although specifying how Graham et al.'s scale can serve as a standard in the field, no claim is being made that this measure should be viewed as the final word. To treat any such measure as sacrosanct would repeat the mistake of the field's failure to assess extant core theoretical scales for decades. Thus, future investigations of the Graham et al. measure should not be stifled but encouraged. In fact, the essence of criminometrics is that scholars must reexamine and update all measures – including those created criminometrically. Such efforts might confirm the merits of the Graham et al. scale or yield a new and improved version. We would welcome either outcome. Arbitrating which measure to use would depend on the relative measurement metrics and performance in explaining behavior.

6.2.2 Implications for Criminology

As with other disciplines, criminology has developed norms regarding acceptable practices within its normal science paradigm. Regarding concept measurement, researchers are expected to use multiple imputations for missing data, scales are to have alphas over 0.70 (Nunnally & Bernstein, 1978), and scale factor loadings are to be more than 0.40 (Ford et al., 1986). Items must have face validity, but the criteria for judging this property are typically generous (e.g., low self-control can be measured by items tapping impulsivity or risk-taking). Single-item measures are discouraged but not excluded; three- or four-item scales are acceptable. In studies involving primary data collection, using measures published in past studies confers legitimacy, even if those scales have not been developed systematically. Inventing new items with strong face validity is allowed, without rigorous analysis assessing whether such additions help or hurt as might be achieved if IRT were used. In secondary analysis, the measurement standards are lower. Scholars are limited to items available in the data set, so two- or three-item scales that seem connected to the concept of interest are acceptable.

Again, no claim is being made that the existing empirical literature is inherently flawed or without value. Still, there are at least three limitations to the current measurement norms in criminology. First, especially in secondary data analysis, the survey items are often used to measure key elements of different theories that they were never intended to measure, making the interpretation of results challenging (Sullivan & McGloin, 2014). For example, in the National Longitudinal Study of Youth (NLSY), Katz (2000) uses parental divorce/separation/remarriage as potential strains experienced by girls. However, Harper and McLanahan (2004) use such variables to measure family structure as a risk for youth incarceration in the context of social control. This same phenomenon of using identical items to measure different constructs has been identified and analyzed in the National Youth Survey (NYS) dataset (Armstrong et al., 2009).

Second, the heterogeneity of measures means that it is difficult to advance the accumulation of knowledge. Different results across studies can be attributed to the use of different measures. This inhibits the ability to assess the status of a theory or causal variable, undermining any attempt at falsification.

Third, current measures are marked by unknown measurement error. It is possible that this error, rather than the limits of theories, contributes to the low to modest explained variance achieved by most criminological perspectives (Weisburd & Piquero, 2008). In fact, in Section 5, we explored this potential, finding that the scale with the worst validity and reliability (by CTT and IRT metrics), the ESS scale, produced the lowest adjusted r-squared values in explaining perceptions of police legitimacy, cooperation with police, and satisfaction with police (see Table 21). As the reliability and validity of a scale improved (e.g., Sunshine and Tyler, 2003a), so too did the adjusted r-squared values. And, with our systematically developed measure – the Graham et al. scale – we were able to explain the most variance for our police legitimacy and cooperation with police models. Therefore, to address the issue of low explained variance, heeding the call of Weisburd and Piquero (2008), improving our measures seems to be a fruitful avenue.

Again, in moving forward, criminology should strive, whenever possible, to incorporate "best practices" in developing measures of constructs. With opt-in surveys available to test iterations of measures, doing so is increasingly feasible. A new subfield should emerge in which scholars will focus on concept development through a systematic psychometric approach. These new measures can then be used in future studies collecting primary data and be included in large studies that will be subject to secondary analysis at a later time. Furthermore, as noted in this Element, it is possible to use new measures – such as our procedural justice scale – to evaluate extant measures' measurement properties and predictive value. The goal would be to have a way to separate better measures from worse ones in studies employing diverse conceptual measures.

Criminologists face a challenge – undertaking more systematic measurement of concepts – that is not in their individual self-interest. As demonstrated here, systematic measurement takes time, broader statistical knowledge, and deep conceptual understanding. Writ large, however, it is in the collective interest of criminology to measure core constructs more systematically, use these scales in ongoing lines of empirical inquiry, and advance knowledge accumulation. Still, we recognize that this change in practices will not occur overnight. Decades of sustained effort are needed to produce a library of criminometrically constructed measures of all criminological constructs. Until this library is more developed, the field is bound to existing measures with unknown psychometric properties.

Beyond calling for a new subfield of criminometrics, three strategies might be employed to improve construct measurement. First, journal editors might begin to incentivize the use of standardized measures by giving preference in publication decisions to research employing such scales. Second, training seminars could be undertaken to give criminologists access to the best measurement practices. Third, as is done by psychology's leading professional organization – the American Psychological Association (APA) – the leading professional organization of criminology, the American Society of Criminology (ASC), could publish a set of recommendations about measurement and the reporting of measurement properties of constructs in published research. Eventually, norms encouraging more rigorous measurement protocols might emerge, making criminometrics the rule rather than the exception.

6.3 Limitations and Future Research

Despite the contribution of its development and use, the Graham et al. scale has some limits to consider, providing an opportunity for future research. First, this measure is intended to reflect global perspectives about procedural justice in policing – not encounter-specific attitudes. Still, global attitudes influence specific attitudes and vice versa (Brandl et al., 1994), so adapting these items to reflect encounter-specific attitudes may be useful. Relatedly, this scale was developed in the context of policing; it is not known if it would generalize into other criminal justice settings (e.g., correctional officers). Future research should address these issues.

Second, this scale does not necessarily capture perceived procedural *injustice.* Based on Section 4's analyses, in which negatively worded items loaded onto an independent factor from positively worded items, procedural injustice may be a distinct construct from procedural justice, or this may reflect methods variance. Nonetheless, when measuring procedural justice, what does it mean to "strongly disagree" to items? Does it mean that respondents are perceiving an *absence* of procedural justice? Or, are respondents perceiving procedural *injustice*? In short, procedural justice and procedural injustice may not be opposing poles on one continuum but two different continuums. Alternatively, this response pattern may reflect stylistic response biases, such as acquiescence bias (e.g., Pickett & Baker, 2014). Future research should examine these issues, exploring the utility of developing a psychometric measure of procedural injustice.

In closing, the importance of the current Element is that it not only contributes a new measure of procedural justice in policing but also serves as a case study for scholars seeking to pursue construct development within criminology. Whatever the value of past measures, a means exists to do better. Using methods outlined here, criminology's research paradigm can develop new and higher standards for measuring constructs. As such, we now open the gates for criminologists to engage in *criminometrics*.

References

Akaike, H. (1974). A new look at the statistical model identification. *IEEE Transactions on Automatic Control, 19*(6), 716–723.

Alreck, P. L., & Settle, R. B. (1985). *The survey research handbook*. Irwin.

Amazon Mechanical Turk. (2018). FAQs. www.mturk.com/worker/help.

American Educational Research Association (AERA), American Psychological Association, & National Council on Measurement in Education. (2014). *The standards for educational and psychological testing*. American Educational Research Association.

American Psychological Association. (2020). Journal article reporting standards (JARS). https://apastyle.apa.org/jars.

Ansolabehere, S., & Schaffner, B. F. (2014). Does survey mode still matter? Findings from a 2010 multi-mode comparison. *Political Analysis*, *22*(3), 285–303.

Antonaccio, O., & Tittle, C. R. (2008). Morality, self-control, and crime. *Criminology*, *46*(2), 479–510.

Armstrong, T. A., Lee, D. R., & Armstrong, G. S. (2009). An assessment of scales measuring constructs in tests of criminological theory based on national youth survey data. *Journal of Research in Crime and Delinquency*, *46*(1), 73–105.

Baker, F. B. (2001). *The basics of item response theory.* Educational Resources Information Center (ERIC) Clearinghouse on Assessment and Evaluation.

Bates, L., Allen, S., & Watson, B. (2016). The influence of the elements of procedural justice and speed camera enforcement on young novice driver self-reported speeding. *Accident Analysis & Prevention*, *92*(1), 34–42.

Becker, M. H. (2021). Deciding to support violence: An empirical examination of systematic decision-making, activism, and support for political violence. *Criminology & Criminal Justice*, *21*(5), 669–686.

Bentler, P. M. (1990). Comparative fit indexes in structural models. *Psychological Bulletin*, *107*(2), 238–246.

Bentler, P. M., & Bonett, D. G. (1980). Significance tests and goodness of fit in the analysis of covariance structures. *Psychological Bulletin*, *88*(3), 588–606.

Bernard, T. J. (1990). Twenty years of testing theories: What have we learned and why? *Journal of Research in Crime and Delinquency*, *27*(4), 325–347.

Bolger, P. C., & Walters, G. D. (2019). The relationship between police procedural justice, police legitimacy, and people's willingness to cooperate with law enforcement: A meta-analysis. *Journal of Criminal Justice*, *60*(1), 93–99.

Brandl, S. G., Frank, J., Worden, R. E., & Bynum, T. S. (1994). Global and specific attitudes toward the police: Disentangling the relationship. *Justice Quarterly, 11*(1), 119–134.

Brown, A. (2018). Item response theory approaches to test scoring and evaluating the score accuracy. In P. Irwing, T. Booth, & D. Hughes (Eds.), *The Wiley handbook of psychometric testing* (pp. 607–638). John Wiley.

Browne, M. W., & Cudeck, R. (1993). Alternative ways of assessing model fit. In K. A. Bollen & J. S. Long (Eds.), *Testing structural equation models* (pp. 136–162). Sage.

Burt, C. H. (2019). Response to "Why longitudinal research is hurting criminology" (March/April 2019) Misguided culprit: Blame bad practices not longitudinal data. *The Criminologist, 44*(4), 13–14.

Canales, R., Gonzalez Magaña, M., Francisco Santini, J., & Cherem Maus, A. (2020). Assessing the effectiveness of procedural justice training for police officers: Evidence from the Mexico City Police. Working paper.

Cattell, J. M. (1890). Mental tests and measurements. *Mind, 15*(59), 373–381.

Chandler, J., Higgins, J. P. T., Deeks, J. J., Davenport, C., & Clarke, M. J. (2017, February). Chapter 1: Introduction. In J. P. T. Higgins, R. Churchill, J. Chandler, & M. S. Cumpston (Eds). *Cochrane handbook for systematic reviews of interventions version 5.2.0*. Cochrane.

Chang, L., & Krosnick, J. A. (2009). National surveys via RDD telephone interviewing versus the internet: Comparing sample representativeness and response quality. *Public Opinion Quarterly, 73*(4), 641–678.

Clark, L. A., & Watson, D. (1995). Constructing validity: Basic issues in objective scale development. *Psychological Assessment, 7*(3), 309–319.

Cliff, N. (1988). The eigenvalues-greater-than-one rule and the reliability of components. *Psychological Bulletin, 103*(2), 276–279.

Collins. (2025). Crisis. www.collinsdictionary.com/dictionary/english/crisis.

Cullen, F. T., Pratt, T. C., & Graham, A. (2019a). Beefing up criminology: Longitudinal research is not the only answer. *The Criminologist, 44*(4), 19–20.

Cullen, F. T., Pratt, T. C., & Graham, A. (2019b). Why longitudinal research is hurting criminology. *The Criminologist, 44*(2), 1–7.

Czapska, J., Radomska, E., & Wójcik, D. (2014). Police legitimacy, procedural justice, and cooperation with the police: A Polish perspective. *Varstvoslovje: Journal of Criminal Justice and Security, 16*(4), 453–470.

Dai, M. (2007). *Procedural justice during police–citizen encounters*. (Doctoral dissertation, University of Cincinnati). Retrieved from ProQuest Dissertations & Theses (UMI Number: 3280116).

Dai, S., Vo, T. T., Kehinde, O. J., He, H., Xue, Y., Demir, C., & Wang, X. (2021). Performance of polytomous IRT models with rating scale data: An investigation over sample size, instrument length, and missing data. *Frontiers in Education*, 6, p. 721963. https://doi.org/10.3389/feduc.2021.721963.

Dawis, R. V. (1987). Scale construction. *Journal of Counseling Psychology, 34* (4), 481–489.

de Ayala, R. J. (1994). The influence of multidimensionality on the graded response model. *Applied Psychological Measurement, 18*(2), 155–170.

de Ayala, R. J. (2009). *The theory and practice of item response theory.* Guilford.

DeVellis, R. F. (2012). *Scale development: Theory and applications (applied social research methods)*. 3rd edition. Sage.

Dillman, D. A., Smyth, J. D., & Christian, L. M. (2014). *Internet, phone, mail, and mixed-mode surveys: The tailored design method*. John Wiley.

DuBois, P. H. (1970). *A history of psychological testing*. Allyn and Bacon.

Eckert, R. (2009). *Community policing as procedural justice: An examination of Baltimore residents after the implementation of a community policing strategy.* (Master's thesis, Villanova University). Retrieved from ProQuest Dissertations & Theses (UMI Number: 1462400).

Elman, B. A. (2013). The civil examination system in late imperial China, 1400–1900. *Frontiers of History in China*, *8*(1), 32–50.

Elliott, I., Thomas, S. D., & Ogloff, J. R. (2011). Procedural justice in contacts with the police: Testing a relational model of authority in a mixed methods study. *Psychology, Public Policy, and Law, 17*(4), 592–610.

Engel, R. S., McManus, H. D., & Herold, T. D. (2020). Does de-escalation training work? A systematic review and call for evidence in police use-of-force reform. *Criminology & Public Policy, 19*(3), 721–759.

European Social Survey. (2011). *Round 5 Module on Trust in the Police and Courts-Question Design Template Draft 1*. Centre for Comparative Social Surveys, City University London.

European Social Survey. (2024). Prospectus. www.europeansocialsurvey.org/sites/default/files/2024-04/prospectus_updated.pdf.

Fancher, R. E. (1998). Biography and psychodynamic theory: Some lessons from the life of Francis Galton. *History of Psychology, 1*(2), 99–115.

Flora, D. B., LaBrish, C., & Chalmers, R. P. (2012). Old and new ideas for data screening and assumption testing for exploratory and confirmatory factor analysis. *Frontiers in Psychology, 3*, Article 55.

Ford, J. K., MacCallum, R. C., & Tait, M. (1986). The application of exploratory factor analysis in applied psychology: A critical review and analysis. *Personnel Psychology, 39*(2), 291–314.

Frank, J., Brandl, S. G., Worden, R. E., & Bynum, T. S. (1996). Citizen involvement in the coproduction of police outputs. *Journal of Crime and Justice*, *19*(2), 1–30.

Furr, M. (2011). *Scale construction and psychometrics for social and personality psychology*. Sage.

Gallup, Inc. (2019). Party affiliation. https://news.gallup.com/poll/15370/partyaffiliation.aspx.

Galton, F. (1879). Psychometric experiments. *Brain*, *2*(2), 149–162.

Gau, J. M. (2011). The convergent and discriminant validity of procedural justice and police legitimacy: An empirical test of core theoretical propositions. *Journal of Criminal Justice*, *39*(6), 489–498.

Gau, J. M. (2014). Procedural justice and police legitimacy: A test of measurement and structure. *American Journal of Criminal Justice*, *39*(2), 187–205.

Gau, J. M. (2015). Procedural justice, police legitimacy, and legal cynicism: A test for mediation effects. *Police Practice and Research*, *16*(5), 402–415.

Gilljam, M., & Granberg, D. (1993). Should we take don't know for an answer? *Public Opinion Quarterly*, *57*(3), 348–357.

Gomes, H. S., Farrington, D. P., Maia, Â., & Krohn, M. D. (2019). Measurement bias in self-reports of offending: A systematic review of experiments. *Journal of Experimental Criminology*, *15*, 313–339.

Gottfredson, M. R., & Hirschi, T. (1990). *A general theory of crime*. Stanford University Press.

Graham, A., Haner, M., Sloan, M. M., Cullen, F. T., Kulig, T. C., & Jonson, C. L. (2020). Race and worrying about police brutality: The hidden injuries of minority status in America. *Victims & Offenders*, *15*(5), 549–573.

Graham, A., Kulig, T. C., & Cullen, F. T. (2019). Willingness to report crime to the police: Traditional crime, cybercrime, and procedural justice. *Policing: An International Journal of Police Strategies and Management*, *43*(1), 1–16.

Graham, A., McManus, H. D., Cullen, F. T., Burton, V. S., Jr., & Jonson, C. L. (2019). Videos don't lie: African Americans' support for body-worn cameras. *Criminal Justice Review*, *44*(3), 284–303.

Graham, A., Pickett, J. T., & Cullen, F. T. (2021). Advantages of matched over unmatched opt-in samples for studying criminal justice attitudes: A research note. *Crime & Delinquency*, *67*(12), 1962–1981.

Graham, A., Pratt, T. C., & McLean, K. (2020). Procedural justice. In C. Chouhy, J. C. Cochran, & C. L. Jonson (Eds.), *Criminal justice theory: Explanations and effects* (Advances in Criminological Theory, Vol. 26, pp. 199–220). Routledge.

Grasmick, H. G., Tittle, C. R., Bursik, R. J., Jr., & Arneklev, B. J. (1993). Testing the core empirical implications of Gottfredson and Hirschi's general theory of crime. *Journal of Research in Crime and Delinquency*, *30*(1), 5–29.

Hambleton, R. K., & Jones, R. W. (1993). Comparison of classical test theory and item response theory and their applications to test development. *Educational Measurement: Issues and Practice*, *12*(3), 38–47.

Hambleton, R. K., Swaminathan, H., & Rogers, H. J. (1991). *Fundamentals of item response theory* (Vol. 2). Sage.

Harkin, D. (2015). Police legitimacy, ideology and qualitative methods: A critique of procedural justice theory. *Criminology & Criminal Justice*, *15* (5), 594–612.

Harper, C. C., & McLanahan, S. S. (2004). Father absence and youth incarceration. *Journal of Research on Adolescence*, *14*(3), 369–397.

Higgins, G. E. (2007). Examining the original Grasmick scale: A Rasch model approach. *Criminal Justice and Behavior*, *34*(2), 157–178.

Hirschi, T. (1969). *Causes of delinquency.* University of California Press.

Holt, T. J., Bossler, A. M., & May, D. C. (2012). Low self-control, deviant peer associations, and juvenile cyberdeviance. *American Journal of Criminal Justice*, *37*, 378–395.

Hu, L. T., & Bentler, P. M. (1999). Cutoff criteria for fit indexes in covariance structure analysis: Conventional criteria versus new alternatives. *Structural Equation Modeling: A Multidisciplinary Journal*, *6*(1), 1–55.

Hunt, T. (1936). The history of measurement in psychology. In T. Hunt, *Measurement in psychology* (pp. 23–56). Prentice-Hall. https://doi.org/10.1037/11336-003.

Ivkovic, S. K. (2014). Police misconduct. In M. D. Resig & R. J. Kane (Eds.) *The Oxford handbook of police and policing* (pp. 302–338). Oxford University Press.

Jackson, J., & Bradford, B. (2010). What is trust and confidence in the police? *Policing: A Journal of Policy and Practice*, *4*(3), 241–248.

Johnson, D., Maguire, E. R., & Kuhns, J. B. (2014). Public perceptions of the legitimacy of the law and legal authorities: Evidence from the Caribbean. *Law & Society Review*, *48*(4), 947–978.

Kaiser, H. F. (1960). The application of electronic computers to factor analysis. *Educational and Psychological Measurement*, *20*(1), 141–151.

Katz, R. S. (2000). Explaining girls' and women's crime and desistance in the context of their victimization experiences: A developmental test of revised strain theory and the life course perspective. *Violence Against Women*, *6*(6), 633–660.

Kempf, K. (1993). The empirical status of Hirschi's control theory. In F. Adler & W. S. Laufer (Eds.), *New directions in criminological theory* (Advances in Criminological Theory, Vol. 4, pp. 143–185). Transaction.

Kempf-Leonard, K. (2019). The status of Hirschi's social control theory after 50 years. In J. C. Oleson & B. Costello (Eds.), *Fifty years of Causes of Delinquency: Criminological essays in honor of Travis Hirschi* (Advances in Criminological Theory, Vol. 25, pp. 161–208). Routledge.

Kim, B., Gerber, J., Henderson, C., & Kim, Y. (2012). Applicability of general power-control theory to prosocial and antisocial risk-taking behaviors among women in South Korea. *The Prison Journal*, *92*(1), 125–150.

Kobayashi, E., Vazsonyi, A. T., Chen, P., & Sharp, S. F. (2010). A culturally nuanced test of Gottfredson and Hirschi's "general theory": Dimensionality and generalizability in Japan and the United States. *International Criminal Justice Review*, *20*(2), 112–131.

Leventhal, G. S. (1980). What should be done with equity theory? New approaches to the study of fairness in social relationships. In K. J. Gergen, M. S. Greenberg, & R. H. Willis (Eds.), *Social exchange: Advances in theory and research* (pp. 27–55). Plenum Press.

Lind, E. A., & Tyler, T. R. (1988). *The social psychology of procedural justice*. Plenum Press.

Loevinger, J. (1957). Objective tests as instruments of psychological theory. *Psychological Reports*, *3*, 635–694.

MacQueen, S., & Bradford, B. (2015). Enhancing public trust and police legitimacy during road traffic encounters: Results from a randomised controlled trial in Scotland. *Journal of Experimental Criminology*, *11*(3), 419–443.

Madon, N. S., Murphy, K., & Williamson, H. (2023). Justice is in the eye of the beholder: A vignette study linking procedural justice and stigma to Muslims' trust in police. *Journal of Experimental Criminology*, *19*(3), 761–783.

Maguire, E. R., & Johnson, D. (2010). Measuring public perceptions of the police. *Policing: An International Journal of Police Strategies & Management*, *33*(4), 703–730.

Masters, E. R. (1974). The relationship between number of response categories and reliability of Likert-type questionnaires. *Journal of Educational Measurement*, *11*(1), 49–53.

Masters, G. N. (1982). A Rasch model for partial credit scoring. *Psychometrika*, *47*(2), 149–174.

Mastrofski, S. D., Jonathan-Zamir, T., Moyal, S., & Willis, J. J. (2016). Predicting procedural justice in police–citizen encounters. *Criminal Justice and Behavior*, *43*(1), 119–139.

Maydeu-Olivares, A. (2015). Evaluating fit in IRT models. In S. P. Reise & D. A. Revicki (Eds.), *Handbook of item response theory modeling: Applications to typical performance assessment* (pp. 111–127). Routledge.

Maydeu-Olivares, A. (2013). Goodness-of-fit assessment of item response theory models. *Measurement: Interdisciplinary Research and Perspectives, 11*(3), 71–101.

Mazerolle, L., Antrobus, E., Bennett, S., & Tyler, T. R. (2013). Shaping citizen perceptions of police legitimacy: A randomized field trial of procedural justice. *Criminology, 51*(1), 33–63.

Mazerolle, L., Bates, L., Bennett, S., White, G., Ferris, J., & Antrobus, E. (2015). Optimising the length of random breath tests: Results from the Queensland Community Engagement Trial. *Australian & New Zealand Journal of Criminology, 48*(2), 256–276.

Mazerolle, L., Bennett, S., Antrobus, E., & Eggins, E. (2012). Procedural justice, routine encounters and citizen perceptions of police: Main findings from the Queensland Community Engagement Trial (QCET). *Journal of Experimental Criminology, 8*(4), 343–367.

Mazerolle, L., Bennett, S., Davis, J., Sargeant, E., & Manning, M. (2013). Procedural justice and police legitimacy: A systematic review of the research evidence. *Journal of Experimental Criminology, 9*(3), 245–274.

Meade, A. W., & Wright, N. A. (2012). Solving the measurement invariance anchor item problem in item response theory. *Journal of Applied Psychology, 97*(5), 1016–1031.

Merriam-Webster. (2025). Crisis. www.merriam-webster.com/dictionary/crisis.

Messick, S. (1995). Validity of psychological assessment: Validation of inferences from persons' responses and performances as scientific inquiry into score meaning. *American Psychologist, 50*(9), 741–749.

Mokken, R. J. (1971). *A theory and procedure of scale analysis*. Mouton.

Murphy, K. (2009). Procedural justice and affect intensity: Understanding reactions to regulatory authorities. *Social Justice Research, 22*(1), 1–30.

Murphy, K. (2023). Encouraging minority trust and compliance with police in a procedural justice experiment: How identity and situational context matter. *Group Processes & Intergroup Relations, 26*(4), 816–832.

Murphy, K., Bradford, B., Sargeant, E., & Cherney, A. (2022). Building immigrants' solidarity with police: Procedural justice, identity and immigrants' willingness to cooperate with police. *British Journal of Criminology, 62*(2), 299–319.

Murphy, K., Hinds, L., & Fleming, J. (2008). Encouraging public cooperation and support for police. *Policing and Society, 18*(2), 136–155.

Murray, K., McVie, S., Farren, D., Herlitz, L., Hough, M., & Norris, P. (2021). Procedural justice, compliance with the law and police stop-and-search: A study of young people in England and Scotland. *Policing and Society, 31* (3), 263–282.

Nägel, C., & Nivette, A. E. (2023). Unexpected events during survey design and trust in the police: A systematic review. *Journal of Experimental Criminology, 19*(4), 891–917.

Nalla, M. K., & Nam, Y. (2021). Corruption and trust in police: Investigating the moderating effect of procedural justice. *International Journal of Offender Therapy and Comparative Criminology, 65*(6–7), 715–740.

Netemeyer, R. G., Bearden, W. O., & Sharma, S. (2003). *Scaling procedures: Issues and applications*. Sage.

Niemi, R. G., Carmines, E. G., & McIver, J. P. (1986). The impact of scale length on reliability and validity: A clarification of some misconceptions. *Quality and Quantity, 20*, 371–376.

Nix, J., Campbell, B. A., Byers, E. H., & Alpert, G. P. (2017). A bird's eye view of civilians killed by police in 2015: Further evidence of implicit bias. *Criminology & Public Policy, 16*(1), 309–340.

Nunnally, J. C. (1975). Psychometric theory: 25 years ago and now. *Educational Researcher, 4*(10), 7–21.

Nunnally, J. C., & Bernstein, I. H. (1978). *Psychometric theory.* McGraw Hill.

Osborne, J. W. (2015). What is rotating in exploratory factor analysis? *Practical Assessment, Research, and Evaluation, 20*(2), 1–8.

Osgood, D. W., McMorris, B. J., & Potenza, M. T. (2002). Analyzing multiple-item measures of crime and deviance I: Item response theory scaling. *Journal of Quantitative Criminology, 18*, 267–296.

Osterlind, S. J., & Everson, H. T. (2009). *Differential item functioning*. Sage.

Paternoster, R., Brame, R., Mazerolle, P., & Piquero, A. (1998). Using the correct statistical test for the equality of regression coefficients. *Criminology, 36*(4), 859–866.

Peer, E., Vosgerau, J., & Acquisti, A. (2014). Reputation as a sufficient condition for data quality on Amazon Mechanical Turk. *Behavior Research Methods, 46*(4), 1023–1031.

Pew Research Center. (2024, May 23). *Public's positive economic ratings slip: Inflation still widely viewed as major problem*. Pew Research Center.

Pickett, J. T., & Baker, T. (2014). The pragmatic American: Empirical reality or methodological artifact? *Criminology, 52*(2), 195–222.

Piquero, A. R., MacIntosh, R., & Hickman, M. (2000). Does self-control affect survey response? Applying exploratory, confirmatory, and item response theory analysis to Grasmick et al.'s self-control scale. *Criminology, 38*(3), 897–930.

Pratt, T. C. (2015). Theory testing in criminology. A. R. Piquero (Ed.), *The handbook of criminological theory* (pp. 37–49). John Wiley.

Pratt, T. C., & Cullen, F. T. (2000). The empirical status of Gottfredson and Hirschi's general theory of crime: A meta-analysis. *Criminology, 38*(3), 931–964.

President's Task Force on 21st Century Policing. (2015). *Final Report of the President's Task Force on 21st Century Policing*. Office of Community Oriented Policing Services.

Psychometric Society (n.d.) *History of the Psychometric Society*. www.psychometricsociety.org/history.

Putnick, D. L., & Bornstein, M. H. (2016). Measurement invariance conventions and reporting: The state of the art and future directions for psychological research. *Developmental Review, 41*, 71–90.

Rebellon, C. J., Trinkner, R., Van Gundy, K. T., & Cohn, E. S. (2019). No guts, no glory: The influence of risk-taking on adolescent popularity. *Deviant Behavior, 40*(12), 1464–1479.

Reisig, M. D., Bratton, J., & Gertz, M. G. (2007). The construct validity and refinement of process-based policing measures. *Criminal Justice and Behavior, 34*(8), 1005–1028.

Rivers, D. (2007, August 1). *Sampling for web surveys*. Prepared for the 2007 Joint Statistical Meetings, Salt Lake City, UT.

Sahin, N. M., Braga, A. A., & Apel, R. (2024). Procedural fairness, socioeconomic status, and driver perceptions of the police during traffic stops: A test of the invariance thesis. *Journal of Experimental Criminology, 20*(4), 1175–1191.

Sahin, N., Braga, A. A., Apel, R., & Brunson, R. K. (2017). The impact of procedurally-just policing on citizen perceptions of police during traffic stops: The Adana randomized controlled trial. *Journal of Quantitative Criminology, 33*(4), 701–726.

Samejima, F. (1969). *Estimation of latent ability using a response pattern of graded scores. Psychometric Monograph No. 17*. Psychometric Society.

Sampson, R. J. (2012). *Great American city: Chicago and the enduring neighborhood effect*. University of Chicago Press.

Sampson, R. J., & Groves, W. B. (1989). Community structure and crime: Testing social-disorganization theory. *American Journal of Sociology, 94* (4), 774–802.

Sampson, R. J., Raudenbush, S. W., & Earls, F. (1997). Neighborhoods and violent crime: A multilevel study of collective efficacy. *Science, 277*(5328), 918–924.

Simmons, A. D., & Bobo, L. D. (2015). Can non-full-probability internet surveys yield useful data? A comparison with full-probability face-to-face surveys in the domain of race and social inequality attitudes. *Sociological Methodology, 45*(1), 357–387.

Simms, L. J. (2008). Classical and modern methods of psychological scale construction. *Social and Personality Psychology Compass*, *2*(1) 414–433.

Singer, L. (2013). London riots: Searching for a stop. *Policing: A Journal of Policy & Practice*, *7*(1), 32–41.

Singleton, R., & Straits, B. (2010). *Approaches to social research*. Oxford University Press.

Spector, P. E. (1992). *Summated rating scale construction: An introduction* (Vol. 82). Sage.

Springer (2024). *Psychometrica: Aim and scope*. https://link.springer.com/journal/11336/aims-and-scope.

Steiger, J. H. (1990). Structural model evaluation and modification: An interval estimation approach. *Multivariate Behavioral Research*, *25*(2), 173–180.

Sullivan, C. J., & McGloin, J. M. (2014). Looking back to move forward: Some thoughts on measuring crime and delinquency over the past 50 years. *Journal of Research in Crime and Delinquency, 51*(4), 445–466.

Sunshine, J., & Tyler, T. R. (2003a). The role of procedural justice and legitimacy in shaping public support for policing. *Law & Society Review, 37*(3), 513–548.

Sunshine, J., & Tyler, T. (2003b). Moral solidarity, identification with the community, and the importance of procedural justice: The police as prototypical representatives of a group's moral values. *Social Psychology Quarterly, 66*(2), 153–165.

Tangney, J. P., Baumeister, R. F., & Boone, A. L. (2004). High self-control predicts good adjustment, less pathology, better grades, and interpersonal success. *Journal of Personality, 72*(2), 271–332.

Têng, S. Y. (1943). Chinese influence on the Western examination system. *Harvard Journal of Asiatic Studies*, *7*(4), 267–312.

Thibaut, J. W., & Walker, L. (1975). *Procedural justice: A psychological analysis*. Lawrence Erlbaum Associates.

Thibaut, J., & Walker, L. (1978). A theory of procedure. *California Law Review, 66*(3), 541–566.

Thissen, D., Pommerich, M., Billeaud, K., & Williams, V. S. (1995). Item response theory for scores on tests including polytomous items with ordered responses. *Applied Psychological Measurement*, *19*(1), 39–49.

Thompson, A. J., & Pickett, J. T. (2020). Are relational inferences from crowdsourced and opt-in samples generalizable? Comparing criminal justice attitudes in the GSS and five online samples. *Journal of Quantitative Criminology, 36*(4), 907–932.

Trinkner, R. (2023). Toward measuring objective procedural justice: Commentary on Terpstra and van Wijck (2022). *Journal of Research in Crime and Delinquency, 60*(3), 378–392.

Trinkner, R., Jackson, J. & Tyler, T. R. (2018). Bounded authority: Expanding "appropriate" police behavior beyond procedural justice. *Law and Human Behavior, 42*(3), 280–293.

Tucker, L. R., & Lewis, C. (1973). A reliability coefficient for maximum likelihood factor analysis. *Psychometrika, 38*(1), 1–10.

Tyler, T. (2017). Procedural justice and policing: A rush to judgment? *Annual Review of Law and Social Science, 13*, 29–53.

Tyler, T. R. (1988). What is procedural justice? Criteria used by citizens to assess the fairness of legal procedures. *Law & Society Review, 22*, 103–136.

Tyler, T. R. (1989). The psychology of procedural justice: A test of the group-value model. *Journal of Personality and Social Psychology, 57*(5), 830–838.

Tyler, T. R. (1990). *Why people obey the law.* Yale University Press.

Tyler, T. R. (2000). Social justice: Outcome and procedure. *International Journal of Psychology, 35*(2), 117–125.

Tyler, T. R. (2004). Enhancing police legitimacy. *Annals of the American Academy of Political and Social Science, 593*(1), 84–99.

Tyler, T. R., & Blader, S. L. (2000). *Cooperation in groups: Procedural justice, social identity, and behavioral engagement*. Psychology Press.

Tyler, T. R., & Folger, R. (1980). Distributional and procedural aspects of satisfaction with citizen–police encounters. *Basic and Applied Social Psychology, 1*(4), 281–292.

Tyler, T. R., & Huo, Y. (2002). *Trust in the law: Encouraging public cooperation with the police and courts*. Russell Sage Foundation.

Tyler, T. R., & Lind, E. A. (1992). A relational model of authority in groups. In *Advances in experimental social psychology* (Vol. 25, pp. 115–191). Academic Press.

Tyler, T., & Nobo, C. (2022). *Legitimacy-based policing and the promotion of community vitality.* Cambridge University Press.

Van Damme, A. (2013). The roots and routes to compliance and citizens' cooperation with the Belgian police. *Journal of Police Studies/Cahiers Politiestudies, 1*(1), 40–63.

Van Damme, A., Pauwels, L., & Svensson, R. (2015). Why do Swedes cooperate with the police? A SEM analysis of Tyler's procedural justice model. *European Journal on Criminal Policy & Research*, *21*(1), 15–33.

van Hall, M., Dirkzwager, A. J., van der Laan, P. H., & Nieuwbeerta, P. (2023). Differential effects of procedural justice? Examining heterogeneity in the perceptions and effects of procedural justice across first-time and recurrent detainees. *Crime & Delinquency*. Advance online, https://doi.org/00111287231155924.

van Veen, F., & Sattler, S. (2020). Modeling updating of perceived detection risk: The role of personal experience, peers, deterrence policies, and impulsivity. *Deviant Behavior*, *41*(4), 413–433.

Walker, J., & Maddan, S. (2008). *Statistics in criminology and criminal justice: Analysis and interpretation*. Jones & Bartlett Learning.

Walters, G. D., & Bolger, P. C. (2019). Procedural justice perceptions, legitimacy beliefs, and compliance with the law: A meta-analysis. *Journal of Experimental Criminology*, *15*(3), 341–372.

Warland, R. H., & Sample, J. (1973). Response certainty as a moderator variable in attitude measurement. *Rural Sociology*, *38*(2), 174–186.

Watkins, M. W. (2018). Exploratory factor analysis: A guide to best practice. *Journal of Black Psychology*, *44*(3), 219–246.

Weems, G. H., & Onwuegbuzie, A. J. (2001). The impact of midpoint responses and reverse coding on survey data. *Measurement and Evaluation in Counseling and Development*, *34*(3), 166–176.

Weisburd, D., & Braga, A. A. (Eds.). (2006). *Police innovation: Contrasting perspectives*. Cambridge University Press.

Weisburd, D., & Piquero, A. R. (2008). How well do criminologists explain crime? Statistical modeling in published studies. *Crime and Justice*, *37*(1), 453–502.

Weisburd, D., Telep, C. W., Vovak, H., Zastrow, T., Braga, A. A., & Turchan, B. (2022). Reforming the police through procedural justice training: A multicity randomized trial at crime hot spots. *Proceedings of the National Academy of Sciences*, *119*(14), e2118780119.

Wikström, P. O. H., & Kroneberg, C. (2022). Analytic criminology: Mechanisms and methods in the explanation of crime and its causes. *Annual Review of Criminology*, *5*, 179–203.

Wood, G., Tyler, T. R., & Papachristos, A. V. (2020). Procedural justice training reduces police use of force and complaints against officers. *Proceedings of the National Academy of Sciences*, *117*(18), 9815–9821.

Worden, R. E., & McLean, S. J. (2017). *Mirage of police reform: Procedural justice and police legitimacy*. University of California Press.

Worden, R. E., McLean, S. J., Engel, R. S., Cochran, H., Corsaro, N., Reynolds, D., . . . & Isaza, G. T. (2020). *The impacts of implicit bias awareness training in the NYPD*. The John F. Finn Institute.

Yang, F. M., & Kao, S. T. (2014). Item response theory for measurement validity. *Shanghai Archives of Psychiatry*, *26*(3), 171–177.

Zwick, W. R., & Velicer, W. F. (1986). Comparison of five rules for determining the number of components to retain. *Psychological Bulletin*, *99*(3), 432–491.

Cambridge Elements

Criminology

About the Series

Elements in Criminology seeks to identify key contributions in theory and empirical research that help to identify, enable, and stake out advances in contemporary criminology. The series focuses on radical new ways of understanding and framing criminology, whether of place, communities, persons, or situations. The relevance of criminology for preventing and controlling crime is also be a key focus of this series.

Cambridge Elements ≡

Criminology

Elements in the Series

A Framework for Addressing Violence and Serious Crime
Anthony A. Braga and David M. Kennedy

Whose "Eyes on the Street" Control Crime? Expanding Place Management into Neighborhoods
Shannon J. Linning and John E. Eck

Confronting School Violence: A Synthesis of Six Decades of Research
Jillian J. Turanovic, Travis C. Pratt, Teresa C. Kulig and Francis T. Cullen

Testing Criminal Career Theories in British and American Longitudinal Studies
John F. MacLeod and David P. Farrington

Legitimacy-Based Policing and the Promotion of Community Vitality
Tom Tyler and Caroline Nobo

Making Sense of Youth Crime: A Comparison of Police Intelligence in the United States and France
Jacqueline E. Ross and Thierry Delpeuch

Toward a Criminology of Terrorism
Gary LaFree

Using the Police Craft to Improve Patrol Officer Decision-Making
James J. Willis and Heather Toronjo

Crime Dynamics: Why Crime Rates Change Over Time
Richard Rosenfeld

The Future of the Criminology of Place: New Directions for Research and Practice
David Weisburd, Barak Ariel, Anthony A. Braga, John Eck, Charlotte Gill, Elizabeth Groff, Clair V. Uding and Amarat Zaatut

Partnerships in Policing: How Third Parties Help Police to Reduce Crime and Disorder
Lorraine Mazerolle, Kevin Petersen, Michelle Sydes and Janet Ransley

The Hidden Measurement Crisis in Criminology: Procedural Justice as a Case Study
Amanda Graham, Francis T. Cullen and Bruce G. Link

A full series listing is available at: www.cambridge.org/ECRM

For EU product safety concerns, contact us at Calle de José Abascal, 56–1°, 28003 Madrid, Spain or eugpsr@cambridge.org.

www.ingramcontent.com/pod-product-compliance
Ingram Content Group UK Ltd.
Pitfield, Milton Keynes, MK11 3LW, UK
UKHW022147080726
473066UK00010B/819

* 9 7 8 1 0 0 9 5 5 8 5 6 3 *